Fear Not

Facing Our Fears Through God's Love

ELM HILL BOOKS
A Division of Thomas Nelson Publishers
Since 1798

www.thomasnelson.com

There is never a fear that has not a corresponding "Fear not."

—Amy Carmichael

Presented to: _____

Presented by: _____

Fear Not: Facing Our Fears Through God's Love ©2005 Elm Hill Books
ISBN: 1-4041-8556-9

For additions, deletions, corrections or clarifications in future editions of this text, please contact Paul Shepherd, Editor in Chief for Elm Hill Books. Email pshepherd@elmhillbooks.com

Products from Elm Hill Books may be purchased in bulk for educational, business, fundraising, or sales promotional use. For information, please email SpecialMarkets@ThomasNelson.com.

Manuscript compiled by Snapdragon Editorial Group, Inc. All stories are used by permission of the author. Unless otherwise marked, Scripture quotations are taken from The Holy Bible, New King James Version. Copyright © 1982 by Thomas Nelson, Inc. Used by permission.

Scripture quotations marked NCV are taken from the International Children's Bible®, New Century Version®. Copyright © 1986, 1988, 1999 by Tommy Nelson™, a division of Thomas Nelson, Inc., Nashville, Tennessee 37214. Used by permission.

Scripture quotations marked TLB are taken from The Holy Bible, The Living Bible Translation. Copyright © 1971. Used by permission of Tyndale House Publishers, Incorporated, Wheaton, Illinois 60189. All rights reserved.

Scripture quotations marked NLT are taken from The Holy Bible, New Living Translation. Copyright © 1996. Used by permission of Tyndale House Publishers, Incorporated, Wheaton, Illinois 60189. All rights reserved.

Scripture quotations marked NIV are taken from the Holy Bible: New International Version® NIV®.(North American Edition)®. Copyright 1973, 1978, 1984 by International Bible Society. Used by permission of Zondervan Publishing House. All rights reserved.

Scripture quotations marked AMP are taken from The Amplified Bible, copyright © 1954, 1958, 1962, 1964, 1965, 1987 by The Lockman Foundation. All rights reserved. Used by permission.

Book Design by Mark Ross / MJ Ross Design

Printed in the United States of America

Dear Friend:

Do you struggle with fear? If so, Fear Not, has been written and compiled just for you. And you. And you. And you. And you! That's right—if you find the world a fearful place to be these days, you are far from alone. Still, giving in to fear will only multiply it and rob you of the joy of living.

God's answer is to fear not. He doesn't expect you to put your head in the sand and pretend that you aren't surrounded by dangers—night and day. But He does want you to consciously and courageously put your fears aside and place your trust in His faithful care.

May your heart be strengthened and your resolve made certain as you read through these pages. Consider carefully the thoughtful writings of great theologians, the stories of everyday people, and the affirmations designed to help you shut out the fears that trouble—and sometimes torment—your heart and mind. May God bless you as you march toward a life of freedom and fearlessness.

—The Publisher

Table of Contents

Fear.

His modus operandi is to manipulate you with the mysterious, to taunt you with the unknown. Fear of death, fear of failure, fear of God, fear of tomorrow—his arsenal is vast. His goal? To create cowardly, joyless souls.

He doesn't want you to make the journey to the mountain. He figures if he can rattle you enough, you will take your eyes off the peaks and settle for a dull existence in the flatlands.

—Max L. Lucado

What Have We to Fear?

❧

**God incarnate is the end of fear;
and the heart that realizes that he is in the midst
will be quiet in the midst of alarm.**

—Frederick Brotherton Meyer

❧

**He has not learned a lesson of life,
who does not every day surmount a fear.**

—Ralph Waldo Emerson

Facing the Fear of Harm

✑

Don't be afraid. Just stand where you are and watch the LORD rescue you.

—Exodus 14:13 NLT

God Keeps Us from Harm

by Hannah Whitall Smith

He has put his angels in charge of you.
They will watch over you wherever you go.
—Psalm 91:11 NCV

If we look at the seen things, we shall not be able to understand the magnitude of God's watchful care or how He keeps us from harm. But the children of God are called to look at the unseen things. "We do not look at the things which are seen, but at the things which are not seen. For the things which are seen are temporary, but the things which are not seen are eternal" (2 Corinthians 4:18). Could we but see with our bodily eyes His unseen forces surrounding us on every side, we would walk through this world in an impregnable fortress, which nothing could ever overthrow or penetrate, for "the angel of the LORD encamps all around those who fear Him, and delivers them" (Psalm 34:7).

We have a striking illustration of this in the history of Elisha as told in 2 Kings of the Bible. The king of Syria was warring against Israel, but his evil designs were continually frustrated by the prophet; and at last he sent his army to the prophet's own city for the express purpose of taking him captive. We read, "The king of Syria sent horses and chariots and a great army there, and they came by night and surrounded the city" (2 Kings 6:14). This was the seen thing.

And the servant of the prophet, whose eyes had not yet been opened to see the unseen things, was alarmed. We read, "And when the servant of the man of God arose early and went out, there was an army surrounding the city with horses and chariots. And his servant said to him, 'Alas, my master! What shall we do?'" (v. 15)

But Elisha could see the unseen things and he answered, "'Do not fear, for those who are with us are more than those who are with them.' And Elisha prayed, and said, 'LORD, I pray, open his eyes that he may see.' Then the LORD opened the eyes of the young man, and he saw. And behold, the mountain was full of horses and chariots of fire all around Elisha" (vv. 16–17).

The presence of God is the fortress of His people. Nothing can withstand it. At His presence the wicked perish; the earth trembles; the hills melt like wax; the cities are broken down; "the heavens also dropped rain at the presence of God; Sinai itself was moved at the presence of God" (Psalm 68:8). And in the secret of this presence He has promised to hide His people from the pride of man and from the strife of tongues. "My Presence will go with you, and I will give you rest" (Exodus 33:14).

I wish it were possible to make every Christian see this truth as plainly as I see it; for I am convinced it is the only way to a completely restful life. Nothing else will enable a soul to live only in the present moment, as we are commanded to do, and to take no thought for tomorrow. Nothing else will take all the risks and "supposes" out of a Christian's heart and enable him to say, "Surely goodness and mercy shall follow me all the days of my life" (Psalm 23:6).

Abiding in God's presence, we run no risks; and such a soul can triumphantly say,

I know not what it is to doubt,

My heart is always gay;

I run no risks, for, come what will,

God always has His way.

There is one text that will take all the "supposes" out of a believer's life, if only it is received and acted out in a childlike faith; it is in Hebrews 13:5–6: "Be content with such things as you have. For He Himself has said, 'I will never leave you nor forsake you.' So we may boldly say: 'The LORD is my helper; I will not fear. What can man do to me?'" (Hebrews 13:6)[1]

≈∞∂

Fear imprisons, faith liberates;
fear paralyzes, faith empowers;
fear disheartens, faith encourages;
fear sickens, faith heals;
fear makes useless, faith makes serviceable—
and most of all,
fear puts hopelessness at the heart of life,
while faith rejoices in its God.

—Harry Emerson Fosdick

The Face of Fear

by Zorene Frazier

I will say of the LORD, "He is my refuge and my fortress;
my God, in Him I will trust." Surely He shall deliver you from
the snare of the fowler . . . He shall cover you with His feathers,
and under His wings you shall take refuge;
. . . You shall not be afraid.
—Psalm 91:2–5

I usually find the quietness of snowfall comforting, but on that evening, I felt a twinge of anxiety as I completed the evening lock-down; put on my coat, hat, and gloves; grabbed my purse and briefcase; and crossed the lobby. Pushing open the heavy doors of our suburban office building, I surveyed the parking lot. It was empty except for the vans from the lawn installation company and my own snow-covered car. The scene looked surreal in the early evening darkness with overhead parking lot lights shining down on the snow. What was I thinking? I must be the only dummy who works late on Friday night, I chided myself.

All I heard as I walked to my car was the crunching of my boots in the snow. Halfway across, I clicked my key to unlock the doors. Then the door was open and I was in! I sat there for a few minutes letting the car warm up and finding a place for my things on the floor of the front seat. It was with a

sense of relief that I put the car in gear and pulled toward the exit, which included a short alleyway down to the street.

It happened as I stopped to look before turning out of the alleyway onto the street—a face out of nowhere, hands banging loudly on my driver's side door. I'll never forget those dark glaring eyes, the open mouth, the dirt-encrusted palms that battered my window. Everything in me said to get out of there. And that's exactly what I did. I floored it, past the exit stop sign and into the street.

Though in retrospect, I can see that the man was probably just a mentally ill member of our homeless population, the incident changed me. I began to obsess about it—expecting to see the man's face, jagged teeth, and grimy hands around every corner, in every dimly lit hallway, and behind every building. I was suddenly afraid to walk across the parking lot alone or ride in my car alone, even take out the trash alone. My life had become complicated and scary.

Things changed one evening when a friend came by. "We're worried about you," she told me. "You don't seem like yourself. Is there anything I can do to help?"

I didn't respond, doubting that she could understand what I was going through. My friend had a large, loving family to watch over her. And most of all, she had a great dad—intelligent, powerful, caring. She had probably never struggled with fear in her life.

My situation was different. My family was scattered around the country, and my father had been dead for a number of years. Even growing up, though, I'd seen little of him. No, I decided. My friend meant well, but she couldn't give me what I really needed—a father to watch over me and chase

away my fears. That sweet friend took no for an answer, but she did insist on praying for me before she left—a prayer that would deliver me from fear.

Later that night, I felt the wetness of my tears on the pillow as I began my nightly prayer. "Our Father, who art in heaven"—I recited as I had countless times before. But as the words passed my lips, I realized I'd never really heard them before. God was a father, my "heavenly" Father. Then a song that the children's choir at church sang began to play in my head, and I could see the children standing there in all their innocence and vulnerability. Their faces were shining, confident, unafraid as their little voices united in praise. Their song was about God being the "heavenly" Father—more intelligent, more powerful, and more caring than any earthly father could ever be.

As the images faded, I became aware of peace—the first I'd known in many weeks. The tightness in my neck and shoulder began to ease, along with the knot in my stomach. I felt warm and loved and safe from harm.

I still live with fear, but I no longer live in fear. Each morning and as many times as it takes during the day, I close my eyes and see myself placing my fears at God's—my Father's—feet. I exchange my fears for His fearlessness. And quite often when some unexpected situation threatens to light a flame of panic in my mind, I hear those children praising our Father and my peace is restored.

Fear Not

Fear knocked at the door.
Faith answered.
No one was there.

—Inscription over mantel of Hinds' Head Hotel, England

What are fears but voices airy?
Whispering harm where harm is not.
And deluding the unwary
Till the fatal bolt is shot!

—William Wordsworth

F.E.A.R.–False Evidence Appearing Real

An Angel in the Closet

by Renie Szilak Burghardt

I, the LORD your God,
will hold your right hand, saying to you,
"Fear not, I will help you."
—Isaiah 41:13

In 1944, as World War II intensified and Tito's communist partisans closed in on the Bàcska region of Hungary, where I was born, my grandparents decided that we should abandon our home near the Serbian border and move to a safer area. So one morning in early fall, we packed a few belongings in our wooden horse-drawn wagon and left behind most of our dear and familiar things.

Hundreds of people packed into wagons just like ours, choking the roadways as we fled the advancing troops. Every time we heard fighter planes approaching, we would scramble out of our wagons and run to take cover in the nearest ditch, praying that those silver cigars above our heads wouldn't drop their bombs on us! At night we would all camp out on the side of the road, building little fires to cook our meager suppers before huddling together in our wagons to get some sleep.

Finally, my grandparents and I settled down again in a city named Zirc, where for a short time we enjoyed relative safety. Even though we had little,

we still celebrated the birth of Christ on His birthday in 1944. But the day after Christmas, our secure world was shattered. That night warplanes could be heard approaching the city. Sirens shrieked their warnings in the darkness as the deafening roar of exploding bombs filled the air. Our house trembled as if it were being shaken in the jaws of some terrible monster!

"The closet! Run into the closet!" an unfamiliar voice urged me. Terror stricken, I ran toward it, while my frantic grandparents followed. When I reached the small closet, I sank down in a corner, covering my ears with my hands, trying to shut out the terrifying noise. Crying, I squeezed my eyes shut so tightly that I didn't think they would ever open again.

"Sweetheart, everything will be all right," my grandmother said, pulling my quaking body into her arms, while my grandfather pulled the closet door shut behind us. The house shuddered and pieces of plaster and dust fell from the ceiling onto our heads as the house began to crumble.

"Grandma, I can't breathe!" I cried out, panic gripping me by the throat. "It's so dark in here! I'm so scared! Are we going to die?"

"Pray, sweetheart, pray. God will protect us," Grandma said, holding me as tightly as possible, while Grandfather shielded us with his own body.

"Dear God, I'm so scared, and I can't breathe," I prayed out loud. "It's so dark in here. Please help us. Please God . . ." On the verge of losing consciousness, my voice trailed off. Suddenly, I felt a soothing touch caress my cheek and I opened my eyes to see a shimmering light. As I reached out toward the light, trying to touch it, my breathing slowed.

"Grandma, do you see the light?" I asked faintly. "It is so beautiful."

"No, sweetheart, I don't see it. But I hear something," she said, her arms still around me.

"There are people out there, digging us out," Grandfather said. "We're in here! We're alive!" he shouted, trying to remove the debris from the inside. Soon, several men pulled us out of the ruins. The bombing had ceased, but all around us houses and buildings had been flattened. We found out later that many had not been as fortunate as we. Lives had been snuffed out in a moment.

Miraculously, our hiding place had stayed mostly intact, even beneath the rubble, and because we stayed in it, our lives were saved.

"What made you run into the closet?" my grandmother asked.

"I heard a voice," I said, still shaking from the experience. "He told me to run into the closet."

"Thank You, God," I heard Grandfather pray, gratefully.

"Your guardian angel was looking out for you," Grandma said, stroking my face. "And he will continue to do so. Don't you ever forget that."

Grandmother's words comforted me, and the terrible fear gripping my heart subsided. Of course, I thought, the Lord sent my guardian angel to help us!

Throughout Scripture, God tells His people, "Fear not!" To this day, whenever fear strikes again, I remember how the Lord sent His angel to a scared little girl in a faraway land, and I know where to turn for help.

Facing the Fear of Loneliness

Fear says, "God may fail me,"
Faith knows He keeps His Word;
"Hitherto the Lord hath helped us;"
Doubting now would be absurd.
Dismiss your doubts and feelings,
"Stand still" and see it through;
And the God who fed Elijah
Will do the same for you.

—Author Unknown

If we possess inward solitude, we will not fear being alone,
for we know that we are not alone.

—Richard J. Foster

Turning the Page

by Elece Hollis

Jesus said, "You can be sure that I will be with you always."
—Matthew 28:20 NCV

The store had finally closed after forty-eight years. A wave of nostalgia washed over me as I walked through the empty space that for so many years had bustled with customers. Through the years, I had watched starry-eyed couples waltz in for engagement rings, young brides excitedly choose china and silver patterns, and husbands ponder strings of pearls and diamond bracelets for Valentine's Day. Teenage girls came to have their ears pierced, and mommies purchased tiny white Bibles with gold-edged pages that I engraved with their babies' names. Students ordered class rings and left with huge grins.

For forty-eight years my husband and I had unlocked the doors each morning; vacuumed the carpets; hung the open sign; and spent the day repairing wrist watches, sizing rings, selling jewelry; and gift-wrapping packages.

For forty-eight years we had eaten our sandwiches, sweet pickles, and potato chips in the back room at lunchtime. We had dusted display cases and shined tea cups and saucers and worked and labored and thrived on the ka-ching-ching of the cash register. Then we'd cleaned up and headed home each night.

I wondered at the brilliant carpet pattern where the display cases had set.

Fear Not

The carpets hadn't seemed faded and old before. The diamond vault stood gaping at me from the back office, waiting for its new owner to retrieve it.

My eyes roamed the walls where once clocks and calendars hung and shelving had held silver and china settings, trinkets, china figurines, cut crystal vases, and fancy candles. They needed painting now, those bare walls covered with lines and shapes of faded colors. The windows stared starkly, void of the advertisements that once had lured passersby into the store.

The store had made a good living for my husband and I. We had done well. What scared me was the loneliness that stretched ahead of me. Running the business had been my habit, my routine, my job for so long. It was my connection to people and friendships and activities.

Remembered laughter rang from the back room and I almost turned to ask, "Milly? Jim, is that you?"

No, silly, I thought to myself and sighed. They aren't here. No one is here. Yet I could almost hear the echoes of boys coming in after school asking for a Coca-Cola and a snack, Livia chattering as she waited for her jewelry to be cleaned, Mr. Reneaau picking up a package for his wife, Jerry telling us he was going off to college, Glen poking his head around the corner to sing out a cheery hello, Merrill's soapy-spongy voice as she waited on customers, and my husband, Arlie's, "Well, not a bad day's work, sweetie. Let's head out."

But they were just memories. I was alone and the door beckoned me to pass through it into my future without the friends and customers I had grown used to seeing each day. That door suddenly looked small and impassable.

I had looked forward to retirement—to resting in front of the fireplace with my feet propped up, reading all those magazines and books I had collected over the years and never found the time for.

Many a harried Christmas season I had dreamed of the day that I would be in this very position, taking down that open sign and heading out the door to the farm to live the life of ease. But what about the people who had filled my days—the "Hey, Miz Hollis," called as a customer came in the door? What about the neighboring business owners; and the vendors and salesmen we had come to know?

In that moment my loneliness overwhelmed me, but I resolutely closed the door and left behind the busy summer and pumpkin-studded autumn of my life to face the season ahead.

"Alone," I found myself repeating in a sing-song way, "Alone, alone, alone—just me—alone." All the way home the words mocked me.

I stopped at the end of the driveway and got out to get the mail. Then I shut off the car and walked out across the yard toward the pond. I wanted to check on the pecans. I wondered if they had started to fall since the first frost—to see if Arlie and I would have a good crop this year.

The tree frogs serenaded me with a chorus of deep throaty chuckles. A squirrel scampered across the path, made it safely to a tree, and clinging to the lowest limb, waved his brown-plumed tail at me, scolding like a disgruntled customer.

From the tallest bald cypress amid the waving strands of gray-green moss, a brrrrrr-whirrrrr of cicadas started up yet another throbbing trill that escalated to a crescendo of sound like music and voices intermingled.

I startled a fishing heron that rose slowly from the shallows and flapped away with an ungainly slow rhythm. "Good-bye!" I yelled after him. I sat down in the grass and slowly tuned in to the music of birds all around me: a woodpecker in the pecan tree, a blue jay scolding from the fence, a cardinal's

flute, and the warble of a meadowlark.

I closed my eyes as a mockingbird performed his repertoire, whistling, warbling, chirping, and singing. I tried to count the number of imitations he performed, but lost track. A ladybug crawled across my hand and a clump of fall flowers turned their bright faces up at me. In a few moments, a late butterfly landed on my sleeve and opened and closed his wings in greeting.

I breathed in deep of that cold, free, full, living air; and suddenly, I knew as long as I was surrounded by God's creation, I would never be lonesome here with so many pleasant voices and so much laughter and music stirring all around me. Here I would move and come and go. Days would dawn, and the sun would set as always.

The winter of my life might prove to be hospitable, comfortable, and cozy after all! Alone compared to the hustle and bustle of our busy shop, but never truly alone. God and His creation would keep me company. Coming inside, I sat down and propped my feet on the ottoman, opened one of those long-awaited books, and turned to a new page.

No, Never Alone

by Ludie D. Pickett

I've seen the lightning flashing,
I've heard the thunder roll.
I've felt sin's breakers dashing,
which almost conquered my soul.
I've heard the voice of my Savior,
bidding me still to fight on.
He promised never to leave me,
never to leave me alone!

The world's fierce winds
are blowing,
temptation sharp and keen.
I have a peace in knowing
my Savior stands between—
He stands to shield me from danger
when my friends are all gone.
He promised never to leave me,
never to leave me alone!

When in affliction's valley
I tread the road of care,
My Savior helps me carry
the cross so heavy to bear;
Though all around me is darkness,
earthly joys all flown;
My Savior whispers His promise,
never to leave me alone!

No, never alone, no never alone,
He promised never to leave me,
He'll claim me for His own;
No, never alone, no never alone.
He promised never to leave me,
Never to leave me alone.[2]

Be able to be alone.
Lose not the advantage of solitude,
but delight to be alone and single with God.
Life is pure flame, and we live by an
invisible sun within us.

—Sir Thomas Browne

Behold, I stand at the door and knock.
If anyone hears My voice and opens the door,
I will come in to him and dine with him,
and he with Me.

—Revelation 3:20

You Have a Friend

by Thomas Watson

Jesus said, "I have called you friends."
—John 15:15

You have a friend in heaven who will never fail you. Solomon said, "There is a friend who sticks closer than a brother" (Proverbs 18:24 NKJV). Such a friend is God. He is very studious and inquisitive on our behalf, He has a debate with Himself, a consulting and projecting on how He may do us good. He is the best friend—one who gives contentment in the midst of all discourtesies of friends.

Consider the following:

(1.) He is a loving friend. The Bible says that God is love. He is said to have engraved us on the palms of His hands (Isaiah 49:16) that we may never be out of His eye. He carries us in His bosom, close to His heart (Isaiah 40:11). There is no stop or stint in His love, but as the river Nile, it overflows all the banks. His love is as far beyond our thoughts, as it is above our deserts. O the infinite love of God, in giving the Son of His love to be made flesh, which was more than if all the angels had been made worms! God in giving Christ to us gave His very heart to us: here is love penciled out in all its glory, and engraved as with the

"spoint of a diamond." All other love is hatred in comparison of the love of our Friend.

(2.) He is a careful friend: We are told that God cares for us (1 Peter 5:7). He minds and transacts our business as His own, and He accounts His people's interests and concernments as His interest. He provides for us, grace to enrich us, glory to ennoble us. A Christian hath a friend who cares for him.

(3.) He is a prudent friend. A friend may sometimes err through ignorance or mistake and give his friend poison instead of sugar; God is skilful as well as faithful. He knows what our disease is and what medication is most proper to apply. He knows what will do us good and what wind will be best to carry us to heaven.

(4.) He is a faithful friend. Most certainly, God is faithful in His promises. Titus 1:2 says, "In hope of eternal life which God, who cannot lie, promised before time began." God's people are "children that will not lie;" but God is a God that cannot lie. He will not deceive the faith of His people. He cannot for He is called "the Truth." He can as easily cease to be God as cease to be true. The Lord may sometimes change His promise, as when He converts a temporal promise into a spiritual one; but He can never break His promise.

(5.) He is a compassionate friend. God's friendship is nothing else but compassion; for there is naturally no affection in us to desire His friendship nor goodness in us to deserve it—the loadstone is in Himself. When we were enemies, He sent an ambassador of peace; when our hearts were turned back from God, His heart was turned toward us.

Oh the tenderness and sympathy of our Friend in heaven! We ourselves have some relenting of heart to those who are in misery; but it is God who gives all the mercies that are in us. Therefore, He is called "the Father of mercies" (2 Corinthians 1:3).

(6.) He is a constant friend: The Scriptures say "his compassions fail not" (Lamentations 3:22 KJV). Friends do often in adversity drop off as leaves in autumn. These are more flatterers than friends. God is a friend forever: "having loved His own who were in the world, He loved them to the end" (John 13:1). Though I feel despised, God loves me. When others cast me away, God loves me to the end. This is enough for me.[3]

Facing the Fear of Loss

❧

*Only positive faith can rout the black menace of fear
and give life a radiance.*

—Marion Hilliard

❧

God is before me,

He will be my guide;

God is behind me,

no ill can betide;

God is beside me,

to comfort and cheer;

God is around me,

so why should I fear?

Little Girl Lost

by Gail M. Hayes

The humble will see their God at work and be glad.
Let all who seek God's help live in joy.
—Psalm 69:32 NLT

Like most parents, I like to think that I handle my children with care. I had been a law enforcement officer during the time when Adam Walsh disappeared, and I knew the face of evil. Working with the police social work unit on cases involving children, I saw and experienced the grim details of missing children every day. It made me a harsh judge of careless parents, who allowed their children to be snatched up by pedophiles.

How could parents lose sight of their own children? How could someone leave a young child unattended? How could someone be so irresponsible? It only took a trip to Wal-Mart to change my mind and humble my pride.

As we entered the Supercenter, we followed our normal routine. My husband and son always shopped together, and my three-year-old daughter and I did the same. It was during these precious moments that my little girl shared the details of her young life and how she viewed the world. We would see a shirt like one worn by one of her classmates or she would spot a toy like one at preschool, and that always prompted a story from her.

After making our usual rounds, we met my husband and son near the front

of the store to check in with one another. None of us was finished shopping, so my husband and son walked away. My daughter missed her daddy and decided to join them. Smiling as I watched the three of them leave together, I turned and continued my own shopping.

Suddenly, without warning, my mother's radar kicked in and I felt an uneasiness I couldn't explain. I quickly located my husband and son and discovered that my daughter was not with them. My husband thought she was with me, and I thought she was with him. Before we could assign blame, I turned into a babbling Daffy Duck!

My husband asked questions, and I shouted and cried. I couldn't answer the simplest inquiry. I couldn't concentrate on anything. Fear and panic rendered me useless, while memories of her tiny hand in mine, her beautiful smile, and her sweet hugs flashed through my mind.

Somewhere in the distance, I heard the faint cries of a child coming from the rear of the store, but I didn't dare stop to investigate, and my husband was nowhere in sight. I couldn't risk leaving the entrance in case a kidnapper tried to sneak out with her. All I knew was that my baby was missing!

As result of Adam Walsh's disappearance, stores nationwide now activate what is known as "Code Adam" to aid in finding missing children. They shut all exits and entrances and search until children are found. If this system had been in place, Adam's abductor would have been caught. Videotapes later showed him leaving the store with Adam. His parents never again saw him alive.

Here I was, a former law enforcement officer who understood the danger better than the average parent, and yet my child was missing. Fear rippled down my spine, and I felt as though I were living a nightmare! When my pride caved in, my experience and training finally kicked in.

I ran to the greeter at the store entrance and explained my situation. To my relief, she said that she remembered my daughter and had not seen her leave the store. She directed me to customer service where they activated a Code Adam. As I heard the voice over the loudspeakers announce my daughter's disappearance, I asked God to forgive my judgmental attitude toward other parents and asked Him to restore my child to me.

By this time, a crowd had gathered and I could sense the tension in the air. Then suddenly, I heard cheers from the crowd and cries coming from the rear of the store. A woman emerged from the crowd, holding my weeping daughter's hand. We threw our arms around each other and cried with joy!

That experience changed me. I had believed something like this couldn't happen to a former cop. I even prayed, read my Bible, and spoke blessings over my children, but there was still an element of pride in all I did. But as the fear of evil gripped my heart, I finally realized that I was not all powerful. I was a flawed human being, who would not always be able to protect my children. I desperately needed—and always will need—God's help and wisdom.

Now when I hear of a missing child, instead of judging the parents, I pray. Instead of questioning their mistakes, I weep. I know all too well that feeling of utter helplessness and fear that comes from losing a child. God, in His infinite mercy, returned my precious daughter to me, but there are others who suffer the ache of permanently losing their children. Because the Lord allowed me to experience the fear of evil, I was humbled and taught lessons I shall not soon forget.

One day, when my daughter hears this story, I pray that she understands the depth of God's love for Her and that His eye is always upon her, even when her mother's back is turned.

∽≈∾

The Lord can clear the darkest skies
Can give us day for night.
Make drops of sacred sorrow rise
To rivers of delight.

—Isaac Watts

I Love Her More

by Belinda Mooney

When you pass through the waters, I will be with you; and through the rivers,
they shall not overflow you. When you walk through the fire, you shall not be
burned, nor shall the flame scorch you. For I am the LORD your God.
—Isaiah 43:2–3

We had only been in Montana for a week when I had to take our fourteen-year-old daughter, Caitlin, to the doctor. It was her right leg again. It had bothered her for about a year, and she had been treated only months before for tendonitis, which helped temporarily. Now, not only was the pain back, but the day before, I had noticed her right leg seemed thinner than her left.

A bit troubled, I called a local clinic. Apparently, they were concerned as well, and we were given an immediate appointment for the next day. Caitlin and I prayed about it, never dreaming it could be anything too serious.

After examining Caitlin's leg, the doctor promptly sent us over to the X-ray department. It disturbed me that she acted so swiftly. Once X-rays were taken, the technician told us the doctor would get back with us. Since it was Friday, we didn't expect to hear anything from her until Monday at the earliest.

Caitlin and I returned to our friend Laurie's house where we were staying temporarily after our move to Montana. Less than two hours later, the doctor called and told me the X-rays revealed a tumor in Caitlin's leg. Butterflies filled

my stomach as I sent a silent prayer for help winging to our heavenly Father.

"Okay," I asked. "What does that mean? What type of tumor?"

"Osteosarcoma," she said. "It's a rare type of cancer that teens can get, usually in the long bones of their arms or legs."

My heart filled with fear at the word cancer. "How do they treat that?" I asked.

"Amputation," she said quietly.

I tried to listen calmly as the doctor explained that she wanted to send Caitlin immediately to a bone specialist to confirm whether it was indeed a cancerous tumor or just an infection in the bone. She would have someone call me to set up an appointment.

My friend Laurie knew something was wrong, and after I hung up the phone, we told the kids we were making a quick trip to Wal-Mart and would be back shortly.

In the van I had a hard time telling Laurie what the doctor had told me. I could hardly speak for the tears, and I still needed to tell my husband, Dale, who was at work. Not Caitlin, Lord, I prayed. She only wants to serve You! I reminded God of how only months before she had committed herself to being a missionary's wife.

Later that evening, Dale and I went for a walk, trying to think things through. We knew the Lord had a purpose for everything. Hadn't He just moved us to Montana to serve Him in a church here? Hadn't He called Dale to the ministry and just seen us through two years of Bible college?

Together, we cried out to God and asked Him to please take care of our daughter. It would break our hearts to lose her! We put Caitlin on every church prayer chain where we knew someone, but still, we withheld our fear from her. We wanted to wait for the final diagnosis.

The next morning, tired after a sleepless, tear-filled night, I left to run errands and continued praying as I drove through town: *Father, Caitlin is Your child too. We dedicated her to You at birth. No matter how serious this is or how sick she becomes, I know she will do Your work. I don't want to lose her, Father, but if her life's work is to spread the Gospel to others through this illness, then so be it. Help us to trust You and be there for her, no matter what the results.*

At that moment, God's Holy Spirit spoke to my fearful heart in a sweet and clear way, saying, *Trust Me. I love her more than you do.*

As His peace surrounded me, I knew God had something wonderful in store for Caitlin, no matter the results of her medical tests.

But later that day my peace was tested when the bone specialist called. Since it was a Saturday, I immediately jumped to conclusions. What doctor ever calls on a Saturday? But this one did! He had looked at Caitlin's X-rays and felt certain it wasn't cancer. He didn't want us to worry all weekend, so he had called. What a precious gift from God!

As it turned out, Caitlin does have a benign tumor on her leg. She takes medication for the pain and should outgrow it in several years. We are so thankful that she is cancer free. We believe the power of prayer had much to with this.

I will always be thankful for the lessons in trust God taught us during this difficult time and for letting me know just how precious our daughter is to Him. Caitlin's future is secure, whether she lives to be fifteen or one hundred. The words He spoke to me that day are ingrained on my heart forever: Trust me. I love her more than you do.

◦◦◦

Anxiety has its use, stimulating us to seek with keener longing for that security where peace is complete and unassailable.

—Saint Augustine of Hippo

Miracle in ICU

by Candace Marra

I cried to him and he answered me! He freed me from all my fears.
—Psalm 34:4 TLB

Because Chad was a miracle baby and an only child, I was obsessed with the fear of losing him, and my paranoia only worsened as he grew older.

Although he was eighteen years old now, it only seemed like yesterday that I was nervously checking his newborn breathing at least once every fifteen minutes. My husband had wanted me to put our son in his own room, but I was too afraid of crib death. For years, I took my son to the doctor for every little sneeze and sniffle, until the poor man told me not to bring Chad back until it was time for his next physical!

My phobic fear of loss was probably the result of suddenly losing my four-year-old brother from undiagnosed pneumonia when I was only twelve. I tried to convince myself that my fears for Chad were unfounded, but it was a tough battle.

Chad never caused us any trouble. He wasn't valedictorian, but he was near the academic top of his class. Even though he was one of the "cool" kids, he still treated everyone with respect, including less popular students. In the youth group, Chad was the all-around wholesome guy whom all the others

looked up to. He was quite athletic too and despite my fear and opposition, he played football, eventually earning a college scholarship. He even talked about playing for the NFL someday. But every time he ran onto the field, I fought my fear that he would be injured.

Then one night it was as if all my nightmares came true! Following graduation, a few kids got drunk, ran a stop sign, and broadsided Chad on his drive home. My son now lay in ICU in critical condition, hooked up to machines and tubes—with broken ribs, a possible punctured lung, and head injuries. What would become of his dreams now?

At the hospital, as I prayed earnestly for Chad, a scripture kept coming to mind: "My grace is sufficient for thee." I didn't want to hear it! I thought God was telling me that Chad was going to die and that His grace would get me through it! I didn't want God's grace—I wanted Chad! My fear turned to anger as I reminded God that Chad was our only child. I told Him I was content to allow His grace to be sufficient for bearing only one child, but that no amount of grace could ever get me through the loss of my beloved son!

I was only allowed in Chad's room for a few minutes each hour. I don't know which was worse—being told it was time to leave or walking in again and seeing him lying so still on those stark white sheets.

In the ICU waiting room, I continued to plead with God. Please, God, tell me he isn't going to die. Send me a sign. Anything! It had been six hours, and Chad still lay in a coma.

There were other people in the waiting room, but I took little notice of them until a doctor came in to talk quietly with another family. After he left, the couple held hands and prayed with such passion and conviction, I knew they were Christians. Desperate for hope, I approached them.

"Will you pray for me?" I stammered. Why did I say that? I wondered. I don't want prayer for me—I want prayer for Chad!

The woman immediately wrapped her arm around me and said, "I thought you looked like you needed prayer."

"Actually, it's my son who needs prayer," I said. "He's in intensive care."

At this point, her husband chimed in, saying, "I'm sure you've been praying for your son all night. Who's praying for you?"

I wanted them to pray for Chad, not me, but all that came out was, "I suppose my husband is." We all turned to look at my husband, who was sleeping uncomfortably in one of the big arm chairs.

The woman smiled and glanced over at her husband. "I think the real reason God brought us here tonight is so we could pray for you," she said.

When we joined hands, their prayers seemed even more passionate than those for their own loved one. It was as if they knew all about me. They prayed about my fear for Chad, even mentioning the "years of fearful thoughts and torment," and my "panic and frustration." To my amazement, they even asked God to show me that His grace was sufficient for me.

After we finished praying, I shared a little about my situation and asked them how they knew to pray that way. They said they hadn't known any of it—they were just praying how they felt God had directed them.

I had prayed and asked God to send me a sign, and He had. Through this wonderful, obedient couple, He had reassured me that He was with me and that He cared deeply about what happened to Chad. For the first time as a mother, I felt at peace about my son. The thick, heavy blanket of burden lifted off my shoulders.

Within minutes, Chad's doctor came to talk to us. "Your son is awake and

asking for you," he said smiling. "Don't worry, he's going to be all right." I reflexively hugged the doctor and turned to tell the other couple our good news, but they were gone. As I rushed to my son's side, I thanked God for His amazing grace and for saving our son's life.

Chad's accident was life-changing—not for him, but for me. Packing the last of my son's belongings as he prepares to leave for college, I look forward to the amazing future God has planned for him. I'm a little sad because I'll miss him, but thanks to God, I'm not afraid to let Him go!

Spelling Love

by Jeannie Branch with Lincoln Rogers

You shall rise before the gray headed and honor the presence of an old man, and
fear your God: I am the LORD.
—Leviticus 19:32

The seventy-seven-year-old Texan's six-foot-four-inch frame couldn't be contained by the shorter hospital bed. All that kept him corralled was the cold, aluminum side rails and the tether of IV lines. Weighing only 138 pounds, my dad would have said he looked like a horse ready for the glue factory.

But when I entered his room, I didn't see the medical equipment, the too-sharp angles of cheekbones, or the way his skin covered his body like a threadbare rug. Instead, I focused on his bright eyes and the broad smile of welcome from my hero and father, the strong and indomitable man who built our large horse barn and finished the interior of our basement with his bare hands.

It was the seventh month of his hospital confinement and time for another of our wonderful visits packed full of comfortable silence, a smattering of small talk, and occasional bits of profound conversation. My therapist husband years ago debunked the myth of quality time.

"There is no such thing as quality time," he said to my surprise. "You can't make up for what you haven't done by cramming gifts, activities, and deep

53

meaningful conversations into bursts of short visits. Do you know how to spell love?" he asked, not waiting for a response, since he was on a roll. "T-i-m-e. Time. Just being in the same room with someone on a consistent basis is real quality time. You can't measure how important it is to someone just to know you're with them under the same roof and available emotionally whenever he or she may need you."

So here I was again, putting those words into practice at the side of my terminally ill father.

Since my husband and I lived in the same town as my parents, we were blessed with the ability to visit my dad in the hospital four or five times a week. Although the routine of the experience could become tedious, driving through heavy Denver traffic, and depressing as we experienced severe illness on every side within the antiseptic halls of the hospital, we never begrudged the actual hours spent at the side of Dad's bed. Each stay was another opportunity for me to put aside my own fears and spell love in the ordinary times we spent together.

Whether it was sharing sections of a newspaper with him in silence, watching TV, playing a game of cards, providing moral support during grueling physical therapy, listening to him and my husband chat about sports, combing his hair, giving him a shave, or planning the details of repairs on the house and garage, each moment kept our relationship strong. He knew by my presence at his side that I loved him.

It wasn't easy. In the beginning it took more than a month to overcome my initial shock and denial that my father was dying. But finally I accepted his drawn-out illness as a gift from God to the family—an opportunity to say all the things that needed saying and to express by my presence how much he

meant to me. Not everyone gets this gift of time before a loved one passes away. Not everyone gets a chance to conquer the fear of losing someone so very special.

A number of years ago, a dear friend's husband died of a heart attack while he was puttering in his workshop, shattering the world as she knew it in the space of a heartbeat. She was devastated and has yet to fully come to grips with her grief and not being able to say good-bye. Even now the fear and pain in her eyes spills out in tears whenever the topic is broached. Over a casual lunch together at a local Mexican restaurant, she said, "You're so blessed to have had time with your father before he died."

Spending time doesn't mean we ignored chances for festive activities. There was a strong urge within me to make sure we celebrated holidays and milestones with small parties in his half of the room, bringing food and laughter as well as taking photos we could share again during a later visit. I'll always remember our "Christmas with the Duke"—a tiny imitation tree, battery operated lights, inexpensive gifts unwrapped on his lap, and a continuous flow of John Wayne movies (Dad's favorite) parading across the television screen in the background.

During our last New Year's Eve together, we wore colorful paper crowns with the year written in bold black marker, blew noisemakers, and popped party favors with miniature surprises inside, in-between various episodes of a Twilight Zone TV marathon. What made those humble parties special were the countless hours spent in quiet support at his bedside, sacrificing a portion of each day to him, conquering our fear of losing him, and spelling love, T-i-m-e.

Through the course of my life, I'm often confronted by pain and anger in individuals who live their lives imprisoned by the fear of loss and the

"could've, would've, should'ves." It's such a freeing and peaceful feeling to look back and know, down to the very core of my soul, that I took advantage of every opportunity God provided me at the end to let my dad know how much I cared.

Before my father went to heaven, he made the difficult decision to enter a hospice facility, passing away in his sleep just a few short weeks after those little Christmas and New Year's parties. I held his fading hand in mine and told him before he left us to say hello to Jesus and that I'd be coming later. The digital photo taken of my father hours before he died has a brilliant flash of light emanating from a corner of the room beside his head. I can't help but wonder if we caught the image of an angel who was sent to take him home.

Dad's memorial service astounded me as hundreds of people celebrated his life by bearing testimony to the time, smiles, and hugs he invested in their lives. I have no regrets whenever a memory of him crosses my mind. I take comfort in knowing that every day of those last seven months were precious gifts from God—unwrapped opportunities to tie up loose ends and to say good-bye to the greatest man I've ever known.

Facing the Fear of Rejection

❧

*The best answer to fear is to have a firm grasp
of what it means to be accepted by God.*

—John Gunstone

❧

*As we are liberated from our fears,
our presence automatically liberates others.*

—William Wordsworth

I Belong to the King

by Ida L. Reed

I belong to the King; I'm a child of His love,

I shall dwell in His palace so fair,

For He tells of its bliss in yon heaven above,

And His children in splendor shall share.

I belong to the King; I'm a child of His love,

And He never forsakes His own.

He will call me someday to His palace above;

I shall dwell by His glorified throne.

I belong to the King, and He loves me I know,

For His mercy and kindness so free

Are unceasingly mine wherever I go,

And my Refuge unfailing is He.

I belong to the King, and His promise is sure:

That we all shall be gathered at last

In His kingdom above, by life's waters so pure,

When this life with its trials is past.

We Must Not Fear

by George MacDonald

The LORD is on my side; I will not fear. What can man do to me?
—Psalm 118:6

We must not fear what others might do to us, but commit our way to the Father of the Family. We must not be anxious to defend ourselves; because God is our defense. But how should we respond when our friends are reviled? God is also their defender as much as ours. Commit your friend's cause also to God who judges righteously. Be ready to bear testimony for your friend, as you would to receive the blow struck at him; but do not plunge into a nest of scorpions to rescue his handkerchief. Be true to him, be sure to show that you love and honor him, but remember that your defense may bring dishonor. Men may say: "What! Is your friend so lacking in self-esteem that he cannot defend himself? Is he unwise enough to drag an expensive veil over a cactus bush?"

Whatever our relation, then, with any peace-breaker, our mercy must ever be within call; and it may help us against an indignation too strong to be pure, to remember that when any man is reviled for righteousness-sake, then is he blessed. [4]

The Words of Others

by Thomas à Kempis

The fear of man brings a snare, but whoever trusts in the LORD shall be safe.
—Proverbs 29:25

Don't take it to heart if some people think badly of you and say unpleasant things about you. You ought to think worse things of yourself and to believe that no one is weaker than yourself. Moreover, if you walk in the spirit you will pay little heed to fleeting words. It is wise to remain silent when accused, to turn inwardly to Me, and not to be disturbed by human opinions.

Do not let your peace depend on the words of others. Their thinking well or badly of you does not make you different from what you are. Where are true peace and glory? Are they not in Me? He who neither cares to please others nor fears to displease them will enjoy great peace, for all unrest and distraction of the senses arise out of disorderly love and vain fear.[5]

Unashamed

by Candace Marra

I am not ashamed of this Good News about Christ.
It is God's powerful method of bringing all who believe it to heaven.
—Romans 1:16 TLB

"Did you hear who's back in town?" my friend Sherry asked over the phone.

"No, who?" I answered.

"Sheila McAndrew!"

I gasped. "You're kidding! Oh, I can't wait to see her! How is she?"

"Still the same old Sheila," Sherry said.

We had all been best friends in high school, but pursued different paths afterward. Sherry went on to college and became a CPA. I married. But Sheila disappeared from our lives after graduation. In the meantime, about five years later, my husband and I gave our lives to Christ at a local revival. Sherry knew I was a Christian, but wanted nothing to do with it.

Sheila had been the clown of our group and could make us laugh until we cried. Life was too short to take seriously, she would say. Back then she thought Christians were "a piece of work"—that they thought they were better than everyone else and just wanted to suck others into their warped thinking. She compared Christianity to drug addiction.

Sherry told me Sheila wanted the three of us to get together for old times'

sake, so we made plans to meet the next day at a local Subway. Before hanging up, Sherry said, "She doesn't know you're a Christian. You might want to keep it that way. She doesn't seem like she's changed much."

My excitement at getting together with an old friend was immediately replaced with a fear of being rejected. I wasn't the same person I had been in high school, and I couldn't pretend I was. I remembered my devotions from a few hours earlier—that we should never be ashamed of the Gospel of Christ. I argued with God that even if I were to tell Sheila I was a Christian, she would never accept Him. Yet I knew my thinking was wrong.

"Oh, God," I prayed, "what am I going to do?" I thumbed through my Bible and came across Psalm 118:6: "The LORD is on my side; I will not fear. What can man do to me?"

True, I thought. Well, what's the worst that could happen? She could ridicule me. Reject me. Refuse to have anything to do with me. She could make a public fool out of me.

I called Brenda, my pastor's wife, and told her I needed prayer. She invited me over for lunch, and after I described my dilemma, her answer was not what I wanted to hear. She believed God had already started preparing me for my meeting with Sheila during my devotional period. She reminded me that it was certainly not hopeless for Sheila to become a Christian and that she deserved the opportunity.

"You have a chance to impact Sheila's eternity," she said. "There's no greater responsibility or privilege than that."

That evening, I talked to my husband about the upcoming reunion, and he agreed with our pastor's wife.

"God never gives us more than we can handle," he reassured me. "He must

think you're strong enough to share your faith. He believes in you, and so do I. I'll pray for you tomorrow during your lunch."

Driving to Subway the next day, I didn't feel strong, but I told God that if He would give me the words to say and the strength to say them, I would obey.

After ordering our sandwiches, Sheila, Sherry, and I started catching up on our lives. Sheila had recently divorced and had come back home to start over. She was studying to become a nurse. My old friend was still her jovial self, but it was obvious life had taken its toll on her. She was impressed with how well Sherry had done for herself.

Then came the dreaded moment when everyone's attention turned to me. I told Sheila about my wonderful marriage and two school-age children.

"I really like my church too," I said, glancing over at Sherry, who shook her head no to avoid the topic. But Sheila jumped on it.

"You don't mean to tell me you're a Christian, do you?" she asked incredulously.

"Actually, Sheila, I am," I managed to say. "Very much so."

She snickered. "Did you know about this?" she asked Sherry, who only nodded. "I don't believe it!" she continued. "You got sucked in! I never would have expected that from you."

"You know, Sheila, when we were kids, I believed what you said about Christians, because I didn't know any better," I said kindly. "But I'm not involved in some strange religion here. I'm friends with God. I don't consider myself better than you or anyone else. I just consider myself fortunate. I wish everyone had what I have."

"Maybe the rest of us are just stronger than you," Sheila bit back. "We can stand on our own."

"I'm sorry you feel that way," I said. "I guess this means we don't have much in common anymore." I rose from my seat, wrote down my phone number, and said, "Call me if you ever change your mind."

I was sad to have lost a friend, but I also felt that I had been obedient to God. That didn't stop me from crying all the way home.

That night Sherry called and told me how impressed she was that I had stood up for myself. She had never known me to be that strong before, and even said she might be open to hearing more about this friendship with God! She had never heard it presented that way before. But our friend Sheila never did call me.

A year later a traveling choir performed at church one Sunday evening. After several choir members gave testimonies about how their lives had been changed by Christ, the director indicated there would be one last testimony from their newest member. I gasped as he announced her name: Sheila McAndrew! I listened in awe as she talked about that pivotal lunch meeting at Subway, followed by a series of difficulties, which ultimately brought her to Christ.

As she finished, we made eye contact, and she winked at me. I haven't seen her since, but I know we have an eternity to look forward to together.

Facing the Fear of the Unknown

Before us is a future all unknown, a path untrod;
Beside us a friend well loved and known—
That friend is God.

—Author Unknown

A Box of Courage

by Cleo Brink

There is no fear in love; but perfect love casts out fear.
—1 John 4:18

Boarding a bus in Lincoln, Nebraska, I was heading off on a great adventure. Janice, Carol, and Stephanie would meet me in Independence, Missouri, the jump-off town for pioneers of yesteryear and now my jumping-off point. We were heading to the Canadian coast of British Columbia for a week of training camp, sort of a boot camp experience, before we were sent to work as summer missionaries on Indian reservations.

I trembled with excitement and nervousness as I hugged my family good-bye. Daddy huddled us together and prayed for me. Then he joked so much that I knew he was anxious about sending me off. He handed me the little Brownie Box camera as he kissed me on my bangs and said, "See you in the fall, sweetie. Love you."

Mama had a box too and a small envelope containing a letter that she instructed me to read later aboard the bus. The box had a key taped to the outside of it, but she said that I should not open the box unless I found myself in a situation where I thought I might not be able to go on.

"Don't forget your seizure medicine and get enough sleep and eat right."

They were afraid for me, an epileptic, going off so far from home for the

first time and to a place where there was no hospital or doctor. If I got sick I would have to come home, yet my parents had never held me back.

"You are the bravest of my girls," Mama told me. "Despite your handicap you have always been courageous and tried hard things."

But as I hugged her good-bye, I wondered if what I was doing was beyond me. I felt a sudden surge of fear as the bus pulled out and I looked back to see Mama and Daddy and my younger siblings waving at the back of the bus.

It wasn't far to Independence—three hours on the Greyhound with stops in small towns along the way. It gave me time to cry and get past the first aches of leaving home and then to argue myself past the doubts and misgivings that were just then—after all the hurrying, scurrying, and packing—surfacing in my mind.

What was I thinking? I wondered. Why on earth would I want to spend a whole summer on a Canadian Indian reservation? What made me think I could do such a thing? I had no idea what to expect. The only Indians I had encountered were in dioramas in a natural-history museum that our fifth-grade teacher had taken us to see. There was a photo of Geronimo and some fierce-looking American Indians in one of those long-ago textbooks. Yet, I had never met an Indian or talked to one face-to-face.

We didn't know which reservation or village we would be sent to or what the people would be like. Would we be in danger? All my life had been stable and according to plan. This was a step into a dark room, a room full of unknowns, where there might be holes in the floor, enemies afoot, dangers lurking.

I hoped, above all, that I wouldn't get sick. I hated the thought that the other girls might have to take care of me. But I was willing to take the risk. I had to know if I was capable of serving in such a foreign setting.

The girls were waiting and we loaded up in Janice's Renault and headed off west. We drove through Nebraska and Wyoming, up and across Montana and the panhandle of Idaho, through Washington and to the Canadian border, where we entered British Columbia and headed for the coast to ferry over to Vancouver Island. The box and the envelope were stowed and forgotten amid all the new sights and sounds.

The training went so quickly that I didn't have time to be fearful or homesick. But it resurfaced when I was told that two of us were being assigned to a small reservation in Washington State. The local schoolteacher had left for the summer and loaned her house. We set to work, teaching sports and hand crafts along with Bible classes, church services, and children's Bible club.

The children accepted us happily. We represented an interesting change of pace from the monotony of the reservation. And I quickly fell in love with the beautiful and inspiring rain forest and north Pacific beaches. It was a shock when Stephanie injured her eye and had to go home where she could get the medical care she needed. I sent her off with smiles and assurances, but inside I felt alone and afraid, with most of the summer still ahead of me. Fear I had tucked way down deep came sprouting up. I couldn't call home and the mail came only occasionally.

It wasn't long until I was rummaging in my duffel bag for the box and the unread letter. The silver key was curious with a tiny green line etched into its stem. I fumbled with it for a good ten minutes before I was rewarded with the pungent scent of cedar as I lifted the lid of the old jewelry box. I was puzzled to find only folded cloth and a few small notes inside.

I took out two starched cotton strips of flowered cloth. I had seen them before; they were the sashes from Mama's best Sunday apron. I laughed at my

mental image of Mama snipping those strings off and pressing them. The message was clear and simple. She had confidence in my abilities and so should I.

Under the sashes was a denim patch from the knee of a child's blue jeans. I'd watched Mama sew dozens of those patches on my brothers' pants as they grew. A note was pinned to the patch.

"Almost everything in life needs patching sooner or later," Mama had written. "Homesickness will heal and mistakes can be patched and mended, so whatever you are facing, don't be afraid to hit it head-on. If you mess up, God can help with the mending."

The next piece in the box was a rectangle from my sister's comforter. We had had those pink-checked gingham spreads for as long as I could remember. I had changed to a more grown-up style awhile back, but my sister hadn't given hers up until shortly before I left home. When I left, she had been busy choosing a replacement.

"Your sister," read the snippet of paper, "has finally settled on a new creamy-white Chenille bedspread. Sometimes, hard decisions have to be made to leave behind things we love, so we can grow up and reach ahead to things we learn to love better. Cut up your old comforters. God will help you make a much better one."

The last piece was the left pocket of Daddy's beloved blue plaid flannel shirt, still attached to a portion of the front. It was pinned with a note. "Sweetie, I can't keep your heart in my pocket anymore. But every morning I put some prayers in God's pocket for you. He will keep you safe and help you do what He has led you to."

The letter, which I read again and again during the weeks ahead, sustained

me through that tough summer—and all the seasons of my life since—read: "Your mama loves you! Your daddy loves you! Your brothers love you! Your sisters love you! God loves you! You are very loved!" I was loved and my fears could not prosper in the face of that truth.

Don't be Afraid of the "Uns" of Life

by Jan White

The Lord alone is my Rock, my rescuer, defense, and fortress—why then should I be tense with fear when troubles come? . . . Trust him all the time. Pour out your longings before him, for he can help!
—Psalm 62:6, 8

Although I've flown many times, I still face the fear factor when it comes to flying. After all, the thousands of planes that land safely every day don't make the evening news. But fear doesn't keep me grounded because I know about the "uns" of life—the "uns" that the airlines tell you about and the "uns" that God wants you to know.

Once passengers find their assigned seats before a flight, a flight attendant begins making announcements. This person tells everyone on board the scheduled airport destination, in case anyone's unintentionally taking the wrong flight. Then she—sometimes, he—demonstrates how to fasten your seatbelt, asking you not to unbuckle it until the pilot says it's okay to move about the cabin.

During the brief information session, passengers are told what to do in case of emergency. If you listen carefully, it's interesting how they describe such a scenario.

In the unlikely event the cabin loses air pressure, an oxygen mask will

drop down from the compartment above your head. The flight attendant holds a mask and shows how the elastic band fits around your head and the mask covers your nose and mouth.

Passengers are instructed to keep their seatbelts fastened while they're seated in case of unexpected turbulence. Whether the flight will travel over land or sea, you learn your seat cushion can be used as a flotation device.

Get the picture? The airlines want passengers to know what to do should the unlikely and unexpected happen.

Often the problems we encounter in life are considered unlikely because they are unexpected, unwanted, and usually come unannounced. With each new day, we face "uns" because life is unpredictable. Ever notice the word "if" is in the center of the word "life?"

The future is uncertain and unknown. From time to time, every one of us will encounter turbulence. Winds of adversity can make life a bumpy journey.

We do not know from day to day when unforeseen circumstances may find us, or a family member, battling an illness or undergoing surgery. Some accidents are unavoidable. A financial crisis may catch us unaware. Unfaithfulness unravels family ties.

During those times, remember we serve a God whose love and power are unlimited. He is unchanging. He's the same "yesterday, today, and forever" (Hebrews 13:8). When things seem uncontrollable to us, remember that God is in control.

The Bible says, "Lean not on your own understanding," (Proverbs 3:5 NKJV). I do not understand aerodynamics and how huge jet planes with lots of people get off the ground and soar into the air, traveling miles above the earth. Likewise, I do not understand when bad things happen to good people. It's

unfair when friends and co-workers undermine you. But when the unthinkable occurs, I do know that the peace God gives passes all my understanding.

When a passenger boards an airplane, they don't sit in the cockpit. Instead, they trust that the pilot's skill and the plane's radar will get them to their destination. The flight attendant asks that electronic devices be turned off, so as not to interfere with the pilot's communication with air traffic controllers.

In the same way, you and I need to put away any unrighteous devices that would hinder our communication with God. Don't let unbelief keep you from the unfailing care and unconditional love of God.

Let God be your pilot, not just co-pilot. He knows all and sees all from His eternal vantage point. Fear causes us to carry excess baggage around with us that we weren't meant to carry. Let go and let God unburden you of whatever weighs you down.

We don't know what may happen today, tomorrow, next week, next month, next year, or during our lifetimes. But we can live unafraid because we know the One who holds the future. We can trust Him to be with us through the journey of life and, in His time, carry us to our eternal destination in heaven.

Comfort in Times of Perplexity

by Charles Spurgeon

I will bring the blind by a way they did not know; I will lead them in paths they
have not known. I will make darkness light before them, and crooked places
straight. These things I will do for them, and not forsake them.
—Isaiah 42:16

The remembrance of our transcendent redemption ought to comfort us in all times of perplexity. When we cannot see our way or we cannot make out what to do, we need not be at all troubled concerning it; for the Lord Jehovah can see a way out of every intricacy. There never was a problem so hard to solve as that which is answered in redemption. Herein was the tremendous difficulty—How can God be just and yet the Savior of sinners? How can He fulfill what He has threatened and yet forgive sin?

If that problem had been left to angels and men, they could never have worked it out throughout eternity; but God has solved it through freely delivering up His own Son. In the glorious sacrifice of Jesus, we see the justice of God magnified; for He laid sin on the blessed Lord, who had become one with His chosen. Jesus identified himself with His people, and therefore their sin was laid upon Him and the sword of the Lord awoke against Him. He was not taken arbitrarily to be a victim, but He was a voluntary Sufferer. His relationship amounted to covenant oneness with His people, and "it behoved

Christ to suffer" (Luke 24:46 KJV). Herein is a wisdom that must be more than equal to all minor perplexities.

Hear this, then, O poor soul in suspense! The Lord says, "I have redeemed you. I have already brought you out of the labyrinth in which you were lost by sin, and therefore I will take you out of the meshes of the net of temptation and lead you through the maze of trial; I will bring the blind by a way that they know not, and lead them in paths that they have not known." Let us commit our way unto the Lord. Mine is a peculiarly difficult one, but I know that my Redeemer lives, and He will lead me by a right way. He will be our Guide even unto death; and after death He will guide us through those tracks unknown of the mysterious region and cause us to rest with Him forever.[6]

The Chosen Path

by Kathryn Lay

The path of the just is like the shining sun,
that shines ever brighter unto the perfect day.
—Proverbs 4:18

Never before had I ever attended such a large memorial service for someone. So many people had turned out to mourn the loss and celebrate the life of my dear friend Linda.

As I sat in the pew, my emotions struggled with the sorrow of losing a special friend, the pain I felt for her husband and four young children, and the horror I felt for her three-year battle against cancer. Yet as I sat there listening to the service, I was blessed by hearing of her strength, her love for God and trust in Him, her care and concern for others in the midst of her pain and fear, and her ability to have planned and written this amazing memorial.

The pastor said something I will never forget: "Linda often said how God had blessed her by teaching her so much through this time. Although she would not have chosen to go down this path, she thanked Him for what this time gave her in her walk with Him and the quality time she spent with her friends and family."

I shivered at the thought. How could my friend have thanked God for lead-

ing her down such a devastating path that ended in her death and separation from her husband and children?

What if God asked me to do something like that—something more difficult than I ever thought I could handle? Yet from painful experience, I knew He asks us to trust Him even when life doesn't make sense and our hearts are bruised and battered.

But what if there were two paths from which to choose? What if Linda had beaten her cancer? What if she had never had cancer at all and been allowed to live a full life? If she had known beforehand that she would grow so much closer to God and her family through the cancer, which path would she have chosen? What path would I choose?

It made me think of my own journey with God. Fifteen years ago, my husband and I decided it was time to start a family after we'd been married for two years. He had finished college and begun his first teaching job, and we were ready. Getting pregnant was the next step on the golden path we planned to walk.

Time went by. Ten years, in fact. Ten years of disappointing pregnancy results, a false pregnancy, painful treatments, jealousy of our friends who were having children, and emotional pain that left us angry and bitter. We prayed and begged God to give us a child, to make us a family. I felt defective and set-apart from other women—terrified that God's plans for us might include leaving us childless.

Then six years ago, through my friend Linda who so recently had died, we were shown a way to adopt a child who had been neglected, abandoned, or abused. Because of Linda's friendship, baby Michelle came into our lives at nine months old, healthy and happy.

I thought about our little girl and the two paths idea. Suppose God had given my husband and me a choice during our time of struggling with infertility and said, "Years down the road, you will adopt a loving, special little girl who will bring you great joy, or, you can have three birth children in the next five years."

My choice would have been to have those three biological children. My patience wouldn't have waited for the promised daughter. I would never have chosen to go through those childless years and then spend another year in classes and being probed and prodded about our lives by strangers.

But I would never go back and change the circumstances. I can't imagine life without my daughter, or the things she's taught us, or the experiences we have gone through as adoptive parents. My prayers would have taken me down an easier path, but God chose a more difficult and fulfilling one for us.

Yet, how can I compare the painful death of my friend to the glorious adoption of my daughter? Only in that Linda and I both came to a crossroads where we had to accept God's will for our lives and conquer our fear.

Would I have chosen such a difficult road for my husband and me to become parents or for my friend's painful death and sure passage into heaven? No, because I could only see the steps in front of me. I couldn't see around God's curves. My fear was of the unknown future.

Thankfully, God doesn't always ask me to choose. Instead, He sets me on the path best followed and gives me the strength to walk it, asking me to hold His hand and trust Him even when I'm afraid. The future is in His hands.

A Prayer

by Thomas à Kempis

I will bless the LORD at all times;
His praise shall continually be in my mouth.
O taste and see that the LORD is good:
blessed is the man that trusteth in him.
—Psalm 34:1, 8 KJV

Lord, what You say is true. Your care for me is greater than all the care I can take of myself. For he who does not cast all his care upon You stands very unsafely. If only my will remain right and firm toward You, Lord, do with me whatever pleases You. For whatever You shall do with me can only be good.

If You wish me to be in darkness, I shall bless You. And if You wish me to be in light, again I shall bless You. If You stoop down to comfort me, I shall bless You; and if You wish me to be afflicted, I shall bless You forever.[7]

Facing the Fear of Death

Fear Not

O death, where is thy sting? O grave, where is thy victory?

—1 Corinthians 15:55 KJV

Christians had lost all fear of death.
Since, therefore, the fear of death is the mother
of all fear, when it has been destroyed,
all other forms of fear are thereby vanquished.

—John Sutherland Bonnell

The fear of death is engrafted in the common nature of all men,
but faith works it out of Christians.

—Vavasor Powell

Consolations against the Fear of Death

by Lewis Bayly

I am persuaded that neither death nor life,
nor angels nor principalities nor powers,
nor things present nor things to come, nor height nor depth,
nor any other created thing,
shall be able to separate us from the love of God
which is in Christ Jesus our Lord.

—Romans 8:38–39

If when you are feeling sick, you find yourself fearful to die, meditate on these truths:

First, for the people of God, there is no death. John 11:26 says: "Whoever lives and believes in Me shall never die. Do you believe this?" When we please God, we are like Enoch, who was translated unto heaven (Genesis 5:24); our pains are like Elijah's fiery chariot that carried him up to heaven (2 Kings 2:11-12) or like the sores of Lazarus that sent him to Abraham's bosom (Luke 16:23). And if many heathen men, such as Socrates, Curtius, Seneca, and others died willingly, when they might have lived, in hope of the immortality of the soul, will you, a child of God called to the marriage-supper of the blessed Lamb (Revelation 19:7), be one of those guests that refuse to go to that joyful banquet? God forbid.

Second, remember that you are already living in the second degree of your

life. You lived nine months in your mother's womb, and then you were of necessity driven out to a fuller life. When that number of months that God has determined for your life here expire, you will have to leave and pass on to the third degree of life in another world, which will never end, which for those who live and die in the Lord, surpasses this life as completely as your life here has surpassed your life in your mother's womb.

Christ himself passed through this door to the last and most excellent degree of life, as have all His saints that lived before you and all who will come after you. Why should you fear something that is common to all God's elect? Why would you not welcome it as so many have before you? Do not fear death, for it is the exodus from one world to a better world—the end of the temporal, but the beginning of eternal life.

Third, there are only three things that can make death seem fearful. 1) the loss of your life here, 2) the pain that you might encounter, 3) something terrible waiting on the other side. All these are false fires and causeless fears.

For the first, if you leave here uncertain goods that thieves may rob, you will find in heaven a true treasure that can never be taken away (Matthew 6:19-20). After all, these things were only lent to you as though you were a steward on account. Your heavenly reward will be forever. If you leave a loving wife, you will be married to Christ, which is more lovely. If you leave children and friends, you will there find all your godly ancestors and children who have previously departed. Yes, Christ, and all His blessed saints and angels, and as many of your children as are God's children, shall follow after you. You leave an earthly possession and a house of clay (2 Corinthians 5:1), but you shall enjoy a heavenly inheritance and a mansion of glory that has been purchased, prepared, and reserved just for you (John 14:2). What have

you really lost? Isn't death really gain? Go home, go home, and we will follow after you.

As for the pain in death, the suffering that comes from fearing death is often worse. And many a Christian dies without any great pangs or pains. Pitch the anchor of your hope on the firm ground of the Word of God, who has promised He will perfect His strength in the midst of your weakness (2 Corinthians 12:9) and will not allow you to be tempted more than you are able to bear (1 Corinthians 10:13). God will shortly turn all your temporal pains to His eternal joys.

Lastly, do not fear the terrible effects that follow after death. If you are a member of Christ's body, they do not belong to you. Christ by His death has taken away the sting of death for the faithful so that there is now no condemnation for those who are in Christ Jesus (Romans 8:1). Christ protests that those who have everlasting life shall not come into condemnation, but pass from death to life (John 5:24).

The Holy Spirit from heaven says, "'Blessed are the dead who die in the Lord from now on. Yes,' says the Spirit, 'that they may rest from their labors, and their works follow them'" (Revelation 14:13). In respect, therefore, of the faithful, death is swallowed up in victory, and its sting, which is sin and the punishment of it, is taken away by Christ (1 Corinthians 15:54–55). Death is called, in respect to our bodies, a sleep and rest (1 Thessalonians 4:13), in respect to our souls, a going to our heavenly Father, a departing in peace, a removing from this body to go to the Lord, a dissolution of soul and body to be with Christ. What shall I say? "Precious in the sight of the LORD is the death of His saints" (Psalm 116:15). These pains are but your throes and travail to bring forth eternal life.

Who, after all, would not pass through hell to go to paradise? Much more through death. There is nothing after death that you need fear; not your sins, because Christ has paid your ransom; not the Judge, for He is your loving brother; not the grave, for it is the Lord's bed; not hell, for your Redeemer keeps the keys, not the devil, for God's holy angels pitch their tents about you and will not leave you till they bring you to heaven. You are never nearer eternal life; glorify, therefore, Christ by a blessed death. Say cheerfully, "Come, Lord Jesus, for thy servant cometh unto thee. I am willing, Lord, help my weakness."[8]

Triumph

by Henry Ware Jr.

Lift your glad voices in triumph on high,

For Jesus hath risen, and man cannot die;

Vain were the terrors that gathered around Him,

And short the dominion of death and the grave;

He burst from the fetters of darkness that bound Him,

Resplendent in glory to live and to save!

Loud was the chorus of angels on high,

The Savior hath risen, and man shall not die.

Glory to God, in full anthems of joy;

The being He gave us death cannot destroy:

Sad were the life we must part with tomorrow,

If tears were our birthright and death were our end;

But Jesus hath cheered the dark valley of sorrow,

And bade us, immortal, to Heaven ascend:

Lift then your voices in triumph on high,

For Jesus hath risen, and man shall not die.

The Last Laugh

by Lisa A. Crayton

A merry heart makes a cheerful countenance.
—Proverbs 15:13

"What a beautiful smile!" I heard people say as they filed past my father's casket. "What's he laughing about?"

Person after person attending my father's funeral commented on his broad grin. It was obvious that no amount of makeup or handiwork had produced that smile. It was too realistic and so reminiscent of the one my dad often sported right before telling a joke. Ever the clown, Pops had an ever-ready supply of quips, jokes, and wisecracks guaranteed to make even the grumpiest person chuckle.

While some wondered what Pops could smile about after years of battling heart disease and other ailments, I knew his smile was rooted in peace with God. He had often been discouraged by his failing health and despised his weekly dialysis treatments, but before he died, Pops conquered his fear of death.

I still remember the day it happened.

My father, once again experiencing chest pain, an indication that his heart might be failing, was rushed to the hospital. That year he had been in and out of the hospital numerous times. I often accompanied him because my mother

had her hands full caring for my elderly grandmother, who was also battling a life-threatening illness.

That day we weren't sure Pops would make it. Gasping for air, he desperately tried not to panic as his heart beat erratically. But I could tell he was scared. I was scared. I knew my fear was reflected in my eyes because my dad wouldn't look into them. After a while I just closed my eyes and started crying. I didn't want to see my father die. I held back my sobs, but as hot tears flowed freely down my cheeks, I quietly sang the first verse of Psalm 27: "The Lord is my light and salvation—whom shall I fear?"

The song was of little comfort, so I began to pray. But I wasn't sure my fear-filled prayer even reached God's ears. An overwhelming fear dominated that emergency room with its cold cement floors and noisy monitoring equipment. It was audible in the absence of Pops' arsenal of jokes and hearty laughter.

Fear was etched in the lines of tension around his usually smiling mouth and in his work-worn fingers that mercilessly gripped mine. It was clear that his life was hanging in the balance. His eyes bulged with pain. The staccato beeps of the monitoring devices grew louder and more frequent. Sensing death was imminent, my daddy squeezed my fingers one final time, and I nearly lost control.

Suddenly, the examination room door flew open. The ER nurse furtively stepped inside and quickly closed the door. I was glad to see her, thinking she had come to check my father's vital signs. Overwhelmed by Pops rapid decline, I acknowledged her presence with a brief nod, but she didn't waste time speaking. She only responded with a glance my way. With swift strides she walked over to my father's bed and began to pray. She spoke words of healing and prayed that "our faith would not falter." With an amen and a

backward glance, she exited just as quickly as she had entered.

"Who was that?" asked my sister Carla, who had walked in shortly before the nurse finished praying.

"I don't have a clue," I replied, awed by the timing of the nurse's visit.

Glancing at Pops, I was thrilled to see his color slowly returning. His breathing also was much improved. By the time some of my other siblings arrived, peace had invaded the room, squeezing out the fear. Pops was cracking jokes and demanding to go home. He didn't get his way. Instead, he was admitted for a week, but thankfully, he completely recovered.

Several days after Pops' attack, I shared the miraculous circumstances surrounding his recovery with one of my brothers. He was a member of the hospital's security team, but was off-duty the day Pops was admitted. From him I learned that the nurse associated my dad's last name with my brother's. She had come in simply to say hello, but opted for prayer instead.

We were grateful she did. She gave Pops a reason to laugh, even in the face of death. He lived several more years after his miracle, and we often reminisced about his ER experience. By the time Pops lost the battle with heart disease, he no longer feared death. No wonder he could smile on his death bed!

Sure, there were tears at Pops' funeral. But there was also lots of laughter, as family and friends swapped stories about him. Many of us walked away more hopeful than sorrowful.

Nearly a decade later, people still talk about Pops' jokes and his parting smile. In conquering the fear of death, Pops proved that the best laugh is often the last laugh.

Ten Minutes

by David Bond

The steps of a good man are ordered by the LORD, and He delights in his way.
—Psalm 37:23

I hated these weekend conferences. Thankfully, the last meeting finished early, so my wife and I checked out of the hotel and were speeding home just after lunch. It was a beautiful fall Sunday afternoon, so at least the two-hundred-and-fifty-mile ride east on the turnpike would be memorable as it twisted its way through mountains and forests ablaze in their late autumn reds and oranges. As we gazed in silence at the flaming colors, I thought about pioneers in earlier times. No turnpike for them, and of course, no tunnels.

Two lanes merged into one as we approached the last of the turnpike tunnels through the mountains, and I jockeyed for position. These fifty-year-old tunnels had never been widened, but for safety reasons, separate twin tunnels with traffic flowing in the opposite direction, had been constructed instead. All except for this last tunnel—the longest.

As it always did, the fear of dying in a horrible accident overwhelmed me as we neared the tunnel entrance, the heavy steel lane barrier giving way to narrow double-yellow lines, the only separation between the mass of steel and rubber, hurtling toward one another. Instinctively, I tightened my grip on the

steering wheel as the speeding west-bound traffic raced by just inches away.

The air currents in the tunnel from the constant flow of traffic in opposing directions pulled and tugged at the car. We're traveling at sixty miles an hour east, they're traveling sixty miles an hour west, and if someone hits us head-on? That would be like crashing at a hundred and twenty miles an hour, I thought with a touch of nausea. Crashes in these tunnels were rare, but they happened.

The always-wet tiled walls and ceiling and the dim yellowish light inside the tunnel contrasted dramatically with the awesome beauty outside. We were in the middle of the tunnel now; only another minute and we would escape. A big rig came toward us, and I gripped the steering wheel even harder, readying myself for battle against the turbulence it would create in its wake. There, a pull to the left, and then right. Okay, under control. A few beads of sweat dampened my forehead, but I dared not wipe them away.

What would it be like to have a head-on crash with a truck like that? I thought grimly. Instant death? Would I ever know what hit me? I hoped not. I reminded myself that to be absent from the body is to be present with the Lord. Here I was again, questioning the Lord about dying. Why did this fear of death have such a grip on me? A couple of minutes spent in this tunnel seemed like an hour.

The tunnel opening ahead was growing larger and getting brighter. Finally, brilliant sunshine splashed our faces and we squinted as we exited the tunnel. The lanes expanded, and I saw that blessed steel barrier between the east- and west-bound lanes again.

The mountains and tunnels were ten minutes behind us, and we now drove through rolling hills and farmland. The gripping fear I experienced in the tunnel was fading. I quickly glanced at my sleeping wife. Had she felt the

same fear as I? Did she think about head-on car crashes in gruesome detail like I? Did she think about death and about dying as much as I did?

Just then an ambulance sped toward us west-bound with its sirens and lights in emergency response mode, followed by another, and still another. Cars pulled into the slow lane to let them pass as they flew toward what was obviously a major accident. I glanced over at my wife, who was now awake, and she returned my weary gaze.

I stared ahead, seeking solace in the beauty of the land, and prayed, "God, please take care of those people who have been involved in a crash, and thank You that we have been given safety thus far. I pray You will be with us and help us to arrive home safely."

Pulling into the driveway an hour later, I shut off the engine and rubbed my aching hands that had gripped the wheel so tightly.

"You look very tired," my wife said.

I was. "These conferences are tiring," I stated matter-of-factly, "and that turnpike ride—"

"Should we try to make it to church tonight, dear?" she asked.

I hesitated slightly, but said, "Yeah, it might be good for us to put forth the effort and get there this evening. We could get a pizza."

After letting my wife out of the car, I drove to Angelino's. It was crowded as always, and the fresh hot pizza smelled delicious. The memory of my fear in the tunnel was forgotten.

When I walked into the kitchen with the steaming hot pizza, I found my wife sitting in front of the TV, weeping.

The reporters gave the top story a bigger time slot because of its spectacular nature. Two people had been killed earlier that afternoon on the turn-

pike in a head-on collision near a tunnel entrance. A west-bound car had suddenly swerved directly into the path of an east-bound car, causing a major collision. Both drivers were pronounced dead at the scene. The accident had happened less than ten minutes after we had made it through that very spot. We could have left ten minutes later and been the innocent victims, yet for some reason, God saw fit to spare us.

Later that night as I tried to listen to our pastor preach, all I could think about was the tunnel crash. Why not us? Just a short ten-minute difference meant we were alive, and those people were dead.

The pastor concluded his sermon and said, "Before we go home this evening, I wonder if there are any prayer or praise items we can take to the Lord. Anyone?"

I was exhausted, both physically and emotionally, but suddenly I sensed the need to say something. I stood up and began to recall the day's events, and I spoke about my fear of death.

"Why was I so afraid?" I asked. "If God wanted today to be my last day, it would have happened, and I would be in His presence right this very moment. But it wasn't His plan. So here I am, talking to all of you. I'm alive. My wife is alive. I still have a church family, and I apparently still have yet to fulfill some purpose in God's plan."

As I finished speaking, tears welled up in my eyes and my spirit rose. A weight lifted off my shoulders as God helped me deal with my fear of death that night. I knew now that when it was time to go home to His kingdom, He would be in the driver's seat.

Facing the Fear of Failure

∽∾

Of all the passions, fear weakens judgment most.

—Cardinal De Retz

Equal to the Task

by Charles Spurgeon

Jesus said, "My grace is sufficient for you,
for My strength is made perfect in weakness."
—2 Corinthians 12:9

I was lamenting this morning my unfitness for my work and especially for the spiritual warfare to which I am called. A sense of heaviness came over me, but relief came very speedily, for which I thank the Lord. Indeed, I was greatly burdened, but the Lord comforted me. The first verse read at the Sabbath morning service exactly met my case. It is in Isaiah 43:1: "Thus says the LORD, who created you, O Jacob, and He who formed you, O Israel: 'Fear not, for I have redeemed you; I have called you by your name; you are Mine.'" I said to myself, "I am what God created me to be, and I am what He formed me to be, and therefore I must, after all, be the right man for the place where He has put me."

We may not blame our Creator, nor suspect that He has missed His mark in forming an instrument for His work. This should be a great comfort to us. Not only do the operations of grace in the spiritual world yield us consolation, but we are even comforted by what the Lord has done in creation. We are told to cease from our fears; and we do so, once we understand that it is the Lord who made us and not we ourselves, and He will justify His own creating skill by accomplishing through us the purposes of His love. Pray, I beseech you, for me, the weakest of my Lord's servants, that I may be equal to the overwhelming task given me.

We are at times troubled by a sense of our personal insignificance. It seems too much to hope that God's infinite mind should enter into our mean affairs. We make our sorrows great under the vain idea that they are too small for the Lord to notice. I believe that our greatest miseries spring from those little worries that we hesitate to bring to our heavenly Father. Our gracious God puts an end to all such thoughts as these by saying, "Fear not, for I have redeemed you" (Isaiah 43:1). You are not of such small account as you suppose. The Lord would never be wasteful of His sacred expenditure.

He bought you with a price, and therefore He thinks a great deal of you. Listen to what the Lord says: "Since you were precious in My sight, you have been honored, and I have loved you" (Isaiah 43:4). It is amazing that the Lord should think so much of us as to give Jesus for us. Yet God's mind is filled with thoughts of love toward man. We know that His only-begotten Son entered this world and became a man. That man, Christ Jesus, has a name at which every knee shall bow, and He is so dear to the Father that, for His sake, His chosen ones are accepted and are made to enjoy the freest access to Him.[9]

Mission Impossible

by Joyce Ermeling-Heiser

I will sing of the mercies of the LORD forever;
with my mouth will I make known Your faithfulness to all generations.
—Psalm 89:1

Why did I agree to go? I thought, speeding toward home while reviewing my recent conversation with a friend from church. Will I ever learn to say no?

My innocent chat with Glen at the grocery store resulted in another unwanted commitment. Before thinking it through, I'd agreed to provide special music the following week for the group who ministered at the rescue mission. I not only didn't know anything about rescue missions, I wasn't a vocal soloist. I'd sung in large and small vocal groups most of my school years, but sing by myself? Not in this lifetime!

I could have kicked myself for mentioning that I was studying voice at Moody Evening School. That's why he'd asked if I would help. He thought I'd be a great addition to the regular group who went every month to present one of the nightly programs.

Over the next few days I wanted to call and cancel, but I'd been taught to

keep my commitments. Instead, I looked through music and prayed about what to sing. I kept coming back to "I Believe in Miracles," a favorite since I'd first heard it sung at church several months before.

Before I knew it, it was Friday and the group headed for the downtown mission. I kept one ear cocked to the conversation around me, but I didn't open my mouth. I was too scared about my upcoming solo and kept chiding myself for agreeing to sing.

The car finally stopped. This can't be it, I thought. This looks like an office. However, the lighted sign on top of the building indicated we were at the right place.

We entered the mission and followed the superintendent up the side aisle and across the front of the auditorium to the prayer room. Petrified, I only glanced at the framed Bible verses hanging on the front and side walls and barely noticed the two grand pianos standing on each side of the platform. The men sat quietly on folding chairs facing the front.

Arriving at the prayer room, my fellow church members tried to put me at ease, knowing this was my first time in a mission. Then each of us prayed for the speaker and special music, but especially for the men attending, that their hearts would be receptive to the gospel message.

All too soon we filed out to the platform. As I sat facing these men, I noticed their dirty and disheveled clothes, matted hair, and unshaven faces. The forlorn, hopeless expressions gripped me. I'd never encountered such despair.

I started asking myself some hard questions. Why were they here? Were they hiding? Was it because of alcohol and drugs? Had they fallen on hard times? With my limited knowledge of rescue missions, I had no answers.

Our leader stood up behind the podium and greeted the homeless men,

asking them to open their song books to a certain page. As the singing started, my apprehension increased.

What am I doing here? I asked myself for the millionth time. I don't belong here. I don't even want to be here!

My solo drew closer with each hymn we sang. As my panic mounted, I began a conversation with the Lord, asking Him what I should do. Then I heard our group leader say, "Joyce, come sing for us."

With shaking knees, I walked to the podium. "Lord, You know the reason I'm here is because I can't say no. It's just You and me now. Please give me the strength I need not to mess up," I pleaded silently.

As I listened to the introduction of my song, my eyes sweeping again over the dejected expressions, an overwhelming desire to share the love of God with these men enveloped me.

I stood a little taller, smiled a little wider, and began to sing, "I Believe in Miracles." My heart's desire was to convey that message. Since accepting Jesus as my personal Savior the year before, I, too, was a miracle—a new creature in Christ. I realized these men needed to hear those words! As I sang that message from my heart, I began to relax.

Relief washed over me as I sat down, and soon my pounding heart returned to its normal rhythm. Leaning back in my chair, I watched and prayed for the men as they listened to the speaker.

Suddenly, an unbidden thought crossed my mind. Will it be easier next time? Next time! Would there be a next time? Did I want there to be? Surprisingly, I realized that I did. In fact, a strong desire now burned in my heart. I wanted to minister in song to the homeless people of Chicago's skid row—men and women I'd known little about just a few hours earlier.

As I had watched the flickers of hope pass over several faces during my song, I felt compelled to come back. Perhaps my music could be a catalyst to help bring the hope of a new life in Christ to these people who seemed to have little or no hope left.

What had seemed an impossible mission that night because of my fear of failure became a possible mission for me with the Lord's courage—a mission and ministry that lasted for twenty years until the skid row area was razed for urban renewal.

The Walk of the Patient One

by Vicki J. Kuyper

I look up to the mountains—does my help come from there?
My help comes from the LORD,
who made the heavens and the earth!
—Psalm 121:1 NLT

I glanced down at my new, purple hiking boots, now caked with two days of dust and mud. They looked like I felt. Tired. Disheveled. On the verge of giving up. I looked up again, exhaling an exhausted sigh. The summit didn't look any closer than it had twenty minutes ago. Maybe Dead Woman's Pass was going to live up to its name.

My stomach lurched as my breakfast threatened to make a second appearance. My lungs, seemingly shrunken to the size of pinto beans, were only able to hold enough breath to sustain me through a single step. With only half the oxygen of sea level available to my over-exerted body, the overall picture was not a pretty one, no matter how picturesque the view.

I shaded my eyes from the sharp morning sun with my grimy hand, surveying the summit, which was shrouded in a bleak, ghostly fog. The line of the Inca Trail cut its way straight up the face of the 13,750-foot mountain peak. Guess the Inca's don't believe in switchbacks like we do back in Colorado. As recently as a week ago, I'd been living the lifestyle of the soft and

disillusioned. Before arriving in Peru, I figured that living over a mile above sea level would help me make this four-day, twenty-three mile trek with relative ease. So much for preconceived notions.

At this moment of truth, the facts were unmistakably clear. I was a forty-year-old mother of two. I was out of shape and had high blood pressure. I would never realize my childhood dream of reaching the fabled Inca city of Machu Picchu. I would die here along the trail, either of altitude sickness or acute embarrassment. The jury was still out on which would be more painful.

Our guide's words from the night before we'd begun our journey echoed in my head. Anyone who gets altitude sickness will have to abandon the trek. I was a disgrace. A weakling. A burden to the rest of the group. Every insecurity I'd ever had about heading off to South America with my extraordinarily fit girlfriend, leaving my "less intrepid" husband and family behind, and actually accomplishing something this demanding at this advanced stage of decay in my life hit me full force. Failure loomed before me like a tangible roadblock, blotting out the last warm rays of hope.

And as for my fellow travelers? They'd already reached the summit, where they were relaxing and enjoying the view—of me the lead-footed straggler a good thirty minutes down the trail. This had been my position since our journey began. Bringing up the rear. Slowly plodding along, alone.

My current humiliation rewound images from the first leg of our trek. A mere ten minutes after we'd left our base camp along the Urumbamba River, tears began to leave muddy trails on my overly red, aerobically-challenged cheeks. Physically and emotionally, I'd been left in the dust.

The Quechua porters had virtually sprinted out of camp ahead of the group. Though they were toting their bodyweight in provisions on their

backs, they seemed as light and free as children out for an afternoon game of catch-me-if-you-can. Tattered leather sandals, instead of high-tech hiking boots, clung loosely to their weathered brown feet. As they ran, their rainbow colored ponchos flapped in the wind like a flock of Peruvian birds flying freely toward the heights of the Andes.

Our guide, Manolo, and his wife adapted a brisk pace alongside my girlfriend and the one other tourist beside myself on this trek. The four chatted easily as they disappeared around the first bend in the trail, leaving me alone and unexpectedly winded. That's when the first of many raindrops began to fall.

What am I doing here? I demanded of God, my only remaining companion. Of course, I already knew the answer. It was the call of a dream. A dream that began in the bookmobile that parked outside of my elementary school. Throughout the third grade, I'd lose myself in the archaeology section, checking out books on ancient cities like Troy, Petra, or Angkor Wat. I'd imagine my future as an archaeologist, as I tenderly uncovered ancient artifacts with my trusty toothbrush. Even then, I knew there was mystery in this world—and I was determined to enter into it. But, out of every story I read and picture I imagined myself part of, it was a photograph of Machu Picchu that ultimately captured my imagination and part of my heart.

The desolate stonework fairyland, perched precariously on the impossibly green cliffs of the Andes, looked like the ultimate childhood fort in my young eyes. A place of wonder and safety. A magical hideaway where a little girl who was afraid of just about everything could finally breathe deeply and find rest. A refuge so close to heaven that maybe, just maybe, she could even touch the face of God . . .

Today, that little girl was taking steps toward making that dream come

true. But, the reality of the road ahead seemed more like a nightmare. Of course, there was the train that ran from Cuzco directly to Machu Picchu in a matter of hours. But, no. That was the way "normal" tourists approached the famous ruins. I wasn't just a tourist. I was a traveler. A sojourner who wanted to fully experience the hidden treasure that I was sure lay on the road less traveled. And here I was on that road, apparently about to die.

My stomach could no longer hold on to my breakfast of hot cereal and coca tea. Chilled and shaking, I leaned against a jagged stone ledge for support and nervously scanned the summit. If no one noticed, maybe I could gather enough strength to keep walking. Maybe I could continue my ongoing charade of being "fine."

But, with the agility of a nimble-footed llama, our guide, Manolo, was already scurrying down the precipitous, rocky trail in my direction, closely followed by one of our porters. The latter carried a canister of oxygen and a first-aid kit. My journey ended here. My charade had been unmasked. As my rescue team approached, I made one last attempt at feigning dignity. I vowed I wouldn't let them see me cry.

In what seemed like a matter of mere minutes, Manolo's hand gently rested on my shoulder, causing me to lift my head and look into his eyes. What I found there surprised me. Compassion. Empathy. Concern. Not a trace of disdain or annoyance.

Manolo accessed my physical condition, his English rising and falling like a mountain stream dancing over the pebbles and boulders of his native tongue. The kindness behind his words soothed the anger that had been building inside of me, anger over my own frailty, anger born in childhood from feeling as though I never quite measured up.

"Do you want to know why you're always last?" Manolo asked quietly. "Because you stop and take pictures. You study the flowers. You observe all the details along the trail. Do you know what I see in the others? They want to reach camp first. They have a goal to accomplish. You have a journey to take. When this trip is over, who will have the most beautiful memories?

"For the last two days, you've been trying to keep up with everyone else. To imitate their pace, instead of trusting in your own. But, God creates each of us differently. You have a pace, and a path, that is different from the rest of the group. Take your eyes off of the others. Focus on the journey God's set before you alone.

"What you need to learn is 'the walk of the patient one.' We don't call it that because others have to be patient with you, but because you have to learn to be patient with yourself. You put one foot one inch in front of the other. Then, do the same thing with the other foot. I know it seems like you're not moving very far or fast, but if you maintain this pace you won't get tired. And you'll make it to the top."

Then, Manolo gave me a choice. He said we could practice "the walk of the patient one" together, making our way toward the summit in silence, or he could tell me stories about the Incas and the Peruvian people as we took our one-inch steps. One choice he did not offer was turning back.

I chose stories, just as I had since childhood ... "The path we now travel was once covered with smooth, white stones, set off by a wildflower border. Five hundred years ago, it was part of a network of roads that extended across the Inca Empire, fifteen thousand miles from Ecuador to Chile. Relay posts were placed several miles apart, so runners could work in tandem to carry messages, and fresh fish for the emperor, from one part of the empire

to another. This Royal Road crossed mountains over twenty thousand feet high, snaked through seemingly impenetrable jungles, and bridged over raging rivers often hundreds of feet across. Wearing white-feathered caps and announcing their arrival with a conch-shell trumpet, messengers made their way over this road at the rate of 250 miles a day . . ."

I found myself lost in another time as Manolo and I made our way, inch-by-inch, up Dead Woman's Pass. I heard stories of rulers, empires, and ancient mysteries of people who worshipped mountains and diligently protected themselves from ghosts. Wildflowers, white feathers, and the rocks on the road all swirled together in my still oxygen-deprived brain. I felt a part of the story, not as one of the runners who so agilely made his way over the very path I was now on, but as a novice explorer. Someone who was just beginning to uncover hidden treasure within myself.

When we finally reached the summit, I was rewarded not only by an encouraging welcome from my fellow travelers, but by a view of what lay beyond the pass. White stone steps, vertigo-inducing in their number and sheer, vertical descent wove their way down through the Valley of the Ghosts and up to the first in a series of snow-dusted mountain peaks—all of which lay between me and my final destination.

I found myself strangely exhilarated. I could hardly wait to move ahead, to see what surprises were waiting along the trail. Even my purple hiking boots seemed oddly refreshed, ready to conquer the next twelve-thousand-foot summit where we were scheduled to stop for a lunch of fruit and fried beets. Upon hearing the menu, my stomach did one final rendition of a quick salsa step, then thankfully settled into silence.

As I drained a bottle of water, I simultaneously drank in the beauty before

me. Besides our small group, there was not another soul in sight. We were alone with it all, with the deeply cragged mountains, the linen-hued valley, the serpentine of stone steps inviting us five hundred years back in time. No one spoke. We seemed tiny, almost trivial, against the immense backdrop of what lay ahead.

"This is the best day of my life!" I blurted out to my girlfriend with whole-hearted joy.

"You're the only person I know who could lose her lunch on the trail and still say that," she responded, with a tone of disbelief.

But, it was true. Something had changed deep within me, freeing me to walk forward alongside my companions without comparison or inner condemnation. To come in last. To overcome my fear of failing. To pursue my dreams with abandon. To enjoy the person God designed me to be.

Dead Woman's Pass had lived up to its name. A part of me had died along the trail that day. I buried it gratefully. Then, without even glancing back, I pointed my purple boots toward the distant peaks and took a confident step toward whatever fresh challenges lay ahead.

∾⧂∽

Victory over fear is the first spiritual duty of man.

—Nicholas Berdyaev

Wings of Faith

by Susan Duke

Blessed is the man who believes in, trusts in, and relies on the Lord, and whose hope and confidence the Lord is.
—Jeremiah 17:7 AMP

All smiles, I waved good-bye to my four writing group friends. My face, however, betrayed my heart. Inside, I was falling apart.

As I drove home, thoughts and emotions spilled out in what seemed like an endless torrent of tears.

"God, if this is Your idea of a joke, I'm not laughing. Can't You see me down here? I can't do this. Just tell me to bail out now and I'll gladly comply. I see the opportunity and don't want to miss it, but I'm just too afraid!"

After several months of my small writing group's casual discussion about possibly writing a book together, we finally decided to go for it and prepare a book proposal. We'd just spent the day critiquing our individual sample chapters and outline. Everyone was excited—except me. I was the new writer, the rookie, the new kid on the block.

Throughout the day, the realization of what was happening consumed my thoughts. Questions kept blinking like neon signs in my head. If this proposal

is accepted, what happens then? What if my writing isn't good enough? What if I can't write under pressure and with a deadline?

I couldn't see a way that I could be part of writing a book about courage when I was so obviously just plain chicken. On the other hand, I didn't want to disappoint my peers, and I didn't want to miss what I knew would be a wonderful opportunity to help launch my writing career. The fact that the proposed book was on the subject of humor was yet another concern. People tell me I'm funny, even hilarious at times, but could I actually write humor? This was not the beginning I'd envisioned.

The tears continued all the way home. To move out of my comfort zone would feel like trying to fly with no wings. I'd been content to this point, blissfully wandering through the enchanted forest of writing, loving every new discovery, sending a story here, an article there. But now I felt as though I'd been snatched from the forest and thrown onto a freeway where I had to run or be run over. I felt anything but strong or courageous. Like an astronaut floating alone in outer space, I felt helpless, terrified.

I needed clear direction.

Once I was safely home in my nest, I wrapped myself in a soft old quilt and curled up like a wounded fledgling on the couch. How could I deal with these strange new emotions that were engulfing me? If I told the group I couldn't do this project with them, I'd feel like a failure. But if I tried and failed, I'd feel even worse.

When my husband, Harvey, arrived home from work that afternoon, he found me waiting pathetically on the couch. Tenderly, he put his arm around me and asked, "What's wrong, honey? Has something happened?"

"Well …" I blurted out, "something's about to happen. I've gotten myself

into an awkward situation, and I don't know how to get out!"

"What on earth are you talking about?" Harvey probed.

As the tears began to fall, I answered, "You know that book my writing group has been talking about? They've decided to do it. I'm going to have to tell my writing friends to count me out. I'm just afraid that I'll let them down and embarrass myself in the process."

The smile on his face did not console me. I was not vying for his sympathy. I was as serious as I'd ever been in my life. "But honey," he said gently, "you can do this. You're a good writer and God is giving you a wonderful opportunity to prove it. And besides, I believe in you. You have nothing to worry about."

I was touched by my husband's kindness, but not convinced.

The next morning, I poured myself a cup of coffee, gathered my Bible and a devotional book, and shuffled out the back door for some quiet time on the deck. Sitting at our patio table, I clutched my coffee cup and held it close, letting the hot steam warm my face. I closed my eyes and listened. A cool breeze swept over me, awakening me to the freshness of the morning. The only sounds I heard were those of birds singing cheerfully as they gathered twigs and leaves for the nests they were building in nearby birdhouses. No anxiety or fear would be troubling these feathered creatures today.

When I opened my eyes, I thought, *My, these little birds seem so focused on their task, creating a safe place of comfort for babies soon to be occupying these cozy nests.*

Suddenly, it was as if a page turned in my heart. I recalled a story I'd once heard about baby birds learning to fly. Mama and daddy birds use feathers and other soft textures, along with twigs, to pad the nest for their newborns.

Once the eggs are hatched and the babies reach a certain stage of growth, the parents begin bringing more twigs and small limbs, deliberately making the crowded nest uncomfortable. It is their not-so-subtle preparation for graduation day—the day Mama Bird shoves them out of the nest and forces them to fly.

I remembered another spring day when I'd had the rare opportunity to observe this rite of passage firsthand. I watched as a baby bird fell to the ground and marveled at the quick response of Mama Bird as she swooped down and gently lifted the baby, coaxing the flapping of its tiny wings to action. I could almost hear her saying, "Come on, you can do it! This is what we birds do! We fly! It's what you were created to do! I believe in you! You must believe too!"

I closed my eyes again, but this time it was to listen to my heart. As God so often does, He used an illustration of nature to show me a simple but magnificent truth. I could almost hear Him whisper, "Do you want to stay in your comfortable nest, or do you believe you can fly?"

I suddenly realized my fear and anxiety were merely growing pains. God was trying to push me out of my comfortable nest in the enchanted writing forest. I smiled to myself, envisioning that even if I fell, He'd be there with an ever-watchful eye, ready to swoop me up, urging me to fly again.

It was graduation day.

I stood to my feet. I held out my arms, flapping invisible wings of faith, and lifted my face heavenward. "Yes, Lord, I believe I can fly!"

That first flight helped me soar above my writing fears of rejection and failure. Now, fourteen books later, I remain forever grateful for the day God gave me my wings of faith.

What Is the Fear of God?

He who fears God need fear nothing else.

—Author Unknown

Be Not Afraid

by Dr. Stanley Allaby

The fear of the LORD is the beginning of knowledge.
—Proverbs 1:7

There is so much to be afraid of in life—war, earthquakes, sickness, financial collapse, crime, and now tsunamis. We're told that sooner or later, a small island on the other side of the globe will complete its slide into the sea, causing a huge tsunami to sweep across the U.S. East Coast. We live in a fear-filled world. So must we also be afraid of God? What does it mean to fear Him?

Many of the world's religions include rites designed to appease the anger of their gods. I once visited a temple in Taiwan and observed a worshiper as he approached the area of the temple where offerings were being presented to his god. Fear was written all over his face. He sounded a large gong. When I asked the reason, my guide said it was "to wake up the god in case he is sleeping." Then the worshiper left fruit, vegetables, and flowers, all in an effort to keep his god from destroying him in a fit of temper.

I have visited among Animists (people who worship the sun, rocks, trees, etc.) in Africa and have seen how they fear their gods, most of which are seen as evil spirits. These people offer chickens and other animals in order to avoid the anger of their deities.

In the Middle Ages there was a great emphasis on judgment and hell as can be seen in much of the art produced during that period. Paintings depict demons torturing people in the flames of hell. During that time even members of Christian churches professed a fear of God's disfavor. The essence of that philosophy was still present in the early days of our country. Preachers like Jonathan Edwards preached sermons that emphasized judgment and depicted a God of anger and wrath.

Today, in secularized America, few people are afraid of God. Most see Him as the almost human manifestation on the popular new show, "Joan of Arcadia." The truth about God can be found somewhere in the middle. He is indeed the almighty God who has the power to destroy us, and there are times when it's appropriate to be afraid of Him.

We should stand in fear of God when we are in rebellion against Him and care little for His commands. Jesus counseled His disciples to fear Him who has power to inflict ultimate punishment on sin. (See Luke 12:5) And the author of the book of Hebrews writes, "If we deliberately keep on sinning after we have received the knowledge of the truth, no sacrifice for sins is left, but only a fearful expectation of judgment and of raging fire that will consume the enemies of God. It is a dreadful thing to fall into the hands of the living God" (Hebrews 10:26-27, 31).

On the other hand, we serve a God who invites us to enter into a fearless, personal relationship with Him. He calls us His children and His friends. The Bible tells us that God has no desire to pin us down and torture us. He loves us and is interested in our happiness and well-being. In fact, the picture God paints in the Bible is one of a caring Father who uses His power to keep us from harm—the harm that comes from living in conflict with our Creator and in

unison with the enemy of our souls, who has sworn to rob, kill, and destroy us. (John 10:10) The fear we are to have for our God is the kind that spurs corrective action and keeps us moving toward the fulfillment of our potential. Our God is not capricious, willful, or cruel. He is loving, kind, and generous.

Are we saying, then, that we should interpret all those references to fear in the Bible—there are 170 in the Old Testament alone and another 13 in the New Testament—in this way? Let's look at the Hebrew—the original language of the Old Testament—for clarification. There are about eight different Hebrew words that can be translated as "fear" in our English Bibles. Seven of those eight words mean "to be afraid, to be pained, to be terrified, or to be frightened." One of those eight words means "to fear in the sense of reverence." This word "yare" is the word used when encouraging us to fear God.

Unger's Bible Dictionary tells us that the fear of God is of several kinds. There is a superstitious fear of God that is the fruit of ignorance and causes people to be afraid that God is a mysterious and malevolent dictator who punishes us for perceived slights. There is a servile fear of God that leads to abstinence from many sins simply because of the dread of punishment. The third type is filial fear of God. This has its spring in love and prompts us not to offend God and to endeavor in all things to please Him. This is not being afraid of God but holding Him in deep and loving reverence. Unger goes on to say, "This fear would subsist in a pious soul were there no punishment of sin. It dreads God's displeasure, desires His favor, reveres His holiness, submits cheerfully to His will, is grateful for His benefits, sincerely worships Him, and conscientiously obeys His commandments."

This filial "fear of God" denotes reverential awe of God's majesty and holiness. Job 37:22–24 (NIV) expresses this truth beautifully: "Out of the north

he comes in golden splendor; God comes in awesome majesty. The Almighty is beyond our reach and exalted in power; in his justice and great righteousness, he does not oppress. Therefore, men revere him, for does he not have regard for all the wise in heart?"

The phrase, "the fear of God," is used in the Bible for these things:

1. The worship of God. "Come, you children, listen to me; I will teach you the fear of the LORD" (Psalm 34:11).

2. The law of God. "The fear of the LORD is clean, enduring forever; the judgments of the LORD are true and righteous altogether" (Psalm 19:9).

The filial "fear of God" is required in the following ways:

1. Keeping God's commandments. "Do not fear; for God has come to test you, and that His fear may be before you, so that you may not sin" (Exodus 20:20).

2. Serving Him and keeping His statutes. "You shall fear the LORD your God and serve Him, and shall take oaths in His name. And the LORD commanded us to observe all these statutes, to fear the LORD our God" (Deuteronomy 6:13, 24).

3. Hearkening to His voice. "If ye will fear the LORD, and serve him, and obey his voice, and not rebel against the commandment of the LORD, then shall ye . . . continue following the LORD your God" (1 Samuel 12:14 KJV).

4. Worshiping in His temple. "I will come into thy house in the multitude of thy mercy: and in thy fear will I worship toward thy holy temple" (Psalm 5:7 KJV).

Fear Not

Great blessing is promised to those who possess the filial "fear of the Lord":

1. The eye of the Lord is on them. "Behold, the eye of the LORD is on those who fear Him, on those who hope is in His mercy" (Psalm 33:18).

2. Angels protect them. "The angel of the LORD encamps all around those who fear Him, and delivers them" (Psalm 34:7).

3. Their lives are lengthened. "The fear of the LORD prolongs days, but the years of the wicked will be shortened" (Proverbs 10:27).

4. They are led to life. "The fear of the LORD is a fountain of life, to turn one away from the snares of death" (Proverbs 14:27).

5. Their desires are fulfilled. "He will fulfill the desire of those who fear Him; He also will hear their cry and save them" (Psalm 145:19).

6. Goodness is bestowed on them. "Oh, how great is Your goodness, which You have laid up for those who fear You" (Psalm 31:19).

7. God's salvation is near them. "Surely His salvation is near to those who fear Him" (Psalm 85:9).

8. Wisdom is bestowed upon them. "The fear of the LORD is the beginning of wisdom" (Proverbs 9:10).

9. Knowledge is bestowed upon them. "The fear of the LORD is the beginning of knowledge" (Proverbs 1:7).

❧

*The fear of the Lord is not a fear of God's
judgments here or hereafter.
It is a reverential affection for God
founded on faith or trust.
It is a fear of offending so good a Being as God is.
The fear of the Lord includes all inward and outward
and private and public worship of God.*

—John Gill

Exposition of the Whole Bible

Martin Luther Discovers the True "Fear of God"

by Dr. Stanley Allaby

Yes, all have sinned; …yet now God declares us "not guilty" of offending him if
we trust in Jesus Christ, who in his kindness freely takes away our sins.
—Romans 3:23–24 TLB

To illustrate this filial "fear of God," we might look at the life of Martin Luther, who was truly a product of the time in which he lived. The theology of the Middle Ages had instilled in him a great fear of God. In addition, he was a highly introspective man and greatly sensitive concerning his sins.

As a young man, Luther was once caught in a severe thunderstorm. The lightning crashed so close to him that he was thrown to the ground. Church historian, Roland Bainton, tells the story:

"On a sultry day in July of the year 1505, a lonely traveler was trudging over a parched road on the outskirts of the Saxon village of Stotternheim. He was a young man, short but sturdy, and wore the dress of a university student. As he approached the village, the sky became overcast. Suddenly there was a shower, then a crashing storm. A bolt of lightning rived the gloom and knocked the man to the ground. Struggling to rise, he cried in terror, 'St. Anne, help me! I will become a monk.'"[10] Thus, motivated by a fear of God, Luther began his life as an Augustinian monk. Fear of a violent death as an

expression of divine judgment and punishment haunted him during his years in the monastery.

Two years after he entered his new life, he was to celebrate Mass for the first time in the chapel. Word had been sent to his father so that the family might attend this most significant occasion. Luther was extremely nervous because of his awesome responsibility. He masked his nervousness quite well during the first part of the Mass, but when he came to the Prayer of Consecration when he would exercise his priestly authority for the first time, he froze at the altar.

R. C. Sproul describes the scene: "He seemed transfixed. His eyes were glassy and beads of perspiration formed on his forehead…his lower lip began to quiver. He was trying to speak the words of the Mass, but no words came forth from his mouth. He went limp and returned to the table where his father and the family guests were seated. He had failed." [11]

Luther offers his own explanation of his experience when he was to say the words, "We offer unto thee, the living, the true, the eternal God." He says, "At these words I was utterly stupefied and terror-stricken. I thought to myself, *With what tongue shall I address such majesty, seeing that all men ought to tremble in the presence of even an earthly prince? Who am I, that I should lift up mine eyes or raise my hands to the divine Majesty? The angels surround Him. At his nod the earth trembles. And shall I, a miserable little pygmy, say, 'I want this, I ask for that'? For I am dust and ashes and full of sin, and I am speaking to the living, eternal and the true God.*"

As a monk, Luther devoted himself to a rigorous kind of austerity. He fasted for days at a time and indulged in severe forms of self-flagellation. He held long prayer vigils, sometimes praying all through the night. He refused

a monk's normal allotment of blankets. He would sometimes lie shivering on his cell floor staring at the crucifix on the wall and crying out for mercy from the God he was sure was angry at him. He did daily confession. He would often stay in the confessional for hours. Once, he spent six hours confessing the sins he had committed the day before. He was so afraid of God that he wanted to make sure no sin in his life was left unconfessed.

At one point his mentor, Staupitz, scolded him: "Man, God is not angry with you. You are angry with God. Don't you know that God commands you to hope?"

Luther was morbid in his guilt and deeply disturbed in his emotions. He was afraid of God. The question that plagued him constantly was, "How can an unjust man survive in the presence of a just God?"

His answer came when he began to study the Scriptures in preparation for his lectures in theology. (He had now become a Doctor of Theology and taught that subject in the University of Wittenburg.) He was studying Paul's epistle to the Romans, and in this study he received a new understanding of God and a new understanding of divine justice. It was an understanding of how God can be merciful without compromising His justice. Here is his description of this experience: "I greatly longed to understand Paul's Epistle to the Romans and nothing stood in the way but that one expression, 'the justice of God,' because I took it to mean that justice whereby God is just and deals justly in punishing the unjust. My situation was that, although an impeccable monk, I stood before God as a sinner troubled in conscience, and I had no confidence that my merit would assuage Him. Therefore, I did not love a just and angry God, but rather hated and murmured against Him. Yet I clung to the dear Paul and had a great yearning to know what he meant.

"Night and day I pondered until I saw the connection between the justice of God and the statement that 'the just shall live by faith.' Then I grasped that the justice of God is that righteousness by which through grace and sheer mercy God justifies us through faith. Thereupon I felt myself to be reborn and to have gone through open doors into paradise. The whole of Scripture took on a new meaning and whereas before the 'justice of God' had filled me with hate, now it became to me inexpressibly sweet in greater love. This passage of Paul became to me a gate of heaven.

"If you have a true faith that Christ is your Savior, then at once you have a gracious God, for faith leads you in and opens up God's heart and will, that you should see pure grace and overflowing love. This it is to behold God in faith that you should look upon His fatherly, friendly heart, in which there is no anger nor ungraciousness. He who sees God as angry does not see Him rightly, but looks only on a curtain as if a dark cloud had been drawn across his face." [12]

When Luther really understood what "The just shall live by faith" really meant, he was no longer afraid of God but entered into the true meaning of "the fear of God"—a loving, reverential awe for the God who loves us so much that "He gave His only begotten Son, that whoever believes in Him should not perish but have everlasting life" (John 3:16).

Are you willing to step out and conquer life's fears as you trust in God and develop in your life "the fear of God"—the one fear that removes all other fears?

Believing Fear

by Andrew Murray

Praise the LORD! Blessed is the man who fears the LORD,
who delights greatly in His commandments.
—Psalm 112:1

The term "fear not" appears in more than one hundred places in the Bible. And yet, in many other places, the word fear is praised as one of the surest tokens of true godliness, acceptable to the Lord, and full of blessings for us. In fact, it says that the people of God bear the name: Those who fear the Lord. The distinction between these two lies in this simple fact: the one is unbelieving fear, the other is believing.

Where fear is found connected with lack of trust in God, there it is sinful and very hurtful. The fear, on the other hand, that is coupled with trust and hope in God, is for the spiritual life entirely indispensable. The fear that has man and what is temporal for its object is condemned. The fear that with childlike confidence and love honors the Father, is commended. It is the believing—not slavish, but filial—fear of the Lord that is presented by the Scriptures as a source of blessing and power. He that fears the Lord will fear nothing else. The fear of the Lord will be the beginning of all wisdom. The fear of the Lord is the sure way to the enjoyment of God's favor and protection.

There are some Christians who by their upbringing are led into the fear of the Lord, even before they come to faith. This is a very great blessing: parents can give no greater blessing than to bring their children up in the fear of the Lord. When those who are thus brought up are brought to faith, they have a great advantage: they are, as it were, prepared to walk in the joy of the Lord. When, on the contrary, others that have not this preparation come to conversion, they have need of special teaching and vigilance, in order to pray for and awaken this holy fear.

The elements of which this fear is composed are many and glorious. The principals are the following:

1. Holy reverence and awe before the glorious majesty of God and before the All Holy. These guard against the superficiality that forgets who God is and that takes no pains to honor Him as God.

2. Deep humility that is afraid of itself and couples deep confidence in God with an entire distrust in itself. Conscious weakness that knows the subtlety of its own heart always dreads doing anything contrary to the will or honor of God. But just because he fears God, such a one firmly reckons on Him for protection. And this same humility inspires him in all his intercourse with his fellowmen.

3. Circumspectness or vigilance. With holy forethought, it seeks to know the right path, to watch against the enemy, and to be guarded against all lightness or hastiness in speech, resolve, and conduct.

4. Holy zeal and courage in watching and striving. The fear of displeasing the Lord by not conducting one's self in everything as His servant, incites to being faithful in that which is least. The fear of the Lord takes

all other fear away and gives inconceivable courage in the certitude
of victory.

Out of this fear is then born joy. "Rejoice with trembling" (Psalm 2:11): the
fear of the Lord gives joy its depth and stability. Fear is the root, joy the fruit:
the deeper the fear, the higher the joy. On this account it is said: "Ye that fear
the LORD, praise him" (Psalm 22:23 KJV); "Ye that fear the LORD, bless the
LORD" (Psalm 135:20 KJV).

Young disciples of Christ, hear the voice of your Father, "Fear the LORD, ye
his saints" (Psalm 34:9 KJV). Let deep fear of the Lord and dread of all that
might displease or grieve Him, fill you. Then shall you never have any evil to
fear. He that fears the Lord and seeks to do all that pleases Him, for him shall
God also do all that he desires. The childlike believing fear of God will lead
you into the love and joy of God, while slavish, unbelieving, cowardly fear is
utterly cast out.

*O my God, unite my heart for the fear of Thy name. May I always be amongst
those that fear the Lord, that hope in His mercy. Amen.*[13]

❧

The only sure way to take fear out of living is to keep a respectful fear of God in our lives, which means to maintain a reverent attitude toward His place and influence in the scheme of things.

—Eugene Asa Carr

❧

O friend, never strike sail to a fear!
Come into port greatly, or sail with God the seas.

—Ralph Waldo Emerson

Affirmations

for

Fearless Living

Those who fear God face life fearlessly.
Those who do not fear God end up fearing everything.

—Richard Christian Halverson

God is our refuge and strength,
A very present help in trouble.
Therefore we will not fear,
Even though the earth be removed,
And though the mountains be carried into
the midst of the sea;
Though its waters roar and be troubled,
Though the mountains shake with its swelling.

—Psalm 46:1–3

Fearless Living

The Bible is God's letter to us, and hidden within its pages—no fewer than fifty-seven times in the King James Version—are the words "fear not" as well as many instances where we are encouraged, "Do not be afraid." It's apparent that He loves us and wants us to surrender our fears in exchange for the security of knowing that we are safe in His mighty hands. In many cases, He has also attached a promise, something positive to hang on to, the gift of a better day.

These beautiful, reassuring scriptures have been personalized and rephrased in the form of affirmations for fearless living—one for each week of the year. The scripture that serves as a basis for each affirmation has been referenced below it. Remember, it's one thing to know God wants you to live fearlessly and another to put it into practice. When you find yourself confronted with fear, take hold of the affirmation for that week, memorize it, meditate on it, own it. Soon you will find yourself growing in faith and fearlessness. God bless you as you embark on your journey to a better life.

WEEK 1

I will **fear not**, for God is my shield and
my exceeding great reward.

GENESIS 15:1

WEEK 2

I will **fear not**, for God has heard my voice.

GENESIS 21:17

WEEK 3

I will **fear not**, for God is with me and will bless me.

GENESIS 26:24

WEEK 4

I will **fear not**, for God's peace envelopes me.

GENESIS 43:23

WEEK 5

I will **fear not**, for I serve the same God who looked
after generations of people before me.

GENESIS 46:3

WEEK 6

I will **fear not**, for God is testing me to see what
I'm made of. I will show Him reverence and
respect that I might resist sin.

EXODUS 20:20

WEEK 7

I will **fear not**, neither will I be discouraged for the Lord
my God has set His promises before me that I
might take hold of them for my own life.

DEUTERONOMY 1:21

WEEK 8

I will **fear not**, neither will my heart be faint.
I will not tremble or be terrified because of my enemies,
for God goes with me to fight for me and to save me.

DEUTERONOMY 20:3–4

WEEK 9

I will be strong and of good courage,
I will fear not, nor be afraid of my enemies:
for the Lord my God goes with me; He will
not fail me, nor forsake me.

DEUTERONOMY 31:6

WEEK 10

> I will **fear not**, nor be dismayed. I will be strong and courageous for the Lord will defeat all my enemies.
>
> JOSHUA 10:25

WEEK 11

> The Lord is my God, I will **fear not**.
>
> JUDGES 6:10

WEEK 12

> I will **fear not** for God will take care of everything I need.
>
> RUTH 3:11

WEEK 13

I will **fear not**; I will go and do what God has told me to do.
He promises that I will never run out of the things I need.

1 KINGS 17:13–14

WEEK 14

I will **fear not** for when I side with God, the two of us
are more powerful than my enemies.

2 KINGS 6:16

WEEK 15

I will be strong and of good courage.
I will **fear not**, nor be dismayed: for the Lord God,
even my God, will be with me; He will not fail me,
nor forsake me, until I have finished all the
work He has called me to do.

1 CHRONICLES 28:20

WEEK 16

*I will **fear not** for God has redeemed me.*
He has called me by my name; I am His.

ISAIAH 43:1

WEEK 17

*When my heart is fearful, I will be strong and **fear not**,*
for my God will come with vengeance,
He will come and save me.

ISAIAH 35:4

WEEK 18

*I will **fear not**, for the Lord, my Redeemer,*
the Holy One will help me.

ISAIAH 41:14

WEEK 19

I do not need to fight in this battle;
I will stand still and see the salvation of the Lord.
*I will **fear not**, nor be dismayed.*
Whenever I come against adversity,
the Lord will be with me.

2 CHRONICLES 20:17

WEEK 20

*I will **fear not**, for God is with me:*
He will bring my children from the east
and gather them from the west.

ISAIAH 43:5

WEEK 21

The Lord who made me and formed me
from my mother's womb will help me;
*therefore, I will **fear not**.*

ISAIAH 44:2

WEEK 22

*I will **fear not** nor be ashamed. I will not be confused nor*
will I be put to shame. For I will forget the shame
of my youth, and never again remember the reproach.

ISAIAH 54:4

WEEK 23

*I will **fear not**, nor be dismayed, for the Lord will save me*
and my children from the dangerous surroundings in
which we live. I will rest and be at ease and
no one will make me afraid.

JEREMIAH 46:27

WEEK 24

God will draw near in the day that I call on Him.
*I will **fear not!** He has pleaded the causes of my soul*
and has redeemed my life.

LAMENTATIONS 3:57–58

WEEK 25

> I will **fear not**, for from the first day that I set my heart
> in prayer and humbled myself before my God,
> my words were heard by Him.
>
> DANIEL 10:12

WEEK 26

> I will **fear not** for God's peace is with me. I have been
> strengthened when He has spoken to me.
>
> DANIEL 10:19

WEEK 27

> I will **fear not**. I will rejoice and be glad for the Lord
> will do great things for me.
>
> JOEL 2:21

WEEK 28

> The Lord will save me and I will be a blessing.
> Therefore, I will **fear not**, and will see that I am
> stronger than I thought I was.
>
> ZECHARIAH 8:13

WEEK 29

> I will **fear not** those who kill the body
> but are unable to kill the soul.
>
> MATTHEW 10:28

WEEK 30

> I will **fear not**, for my prayers are heard.
>
> LUKE 1:13

WEEK 31

*I will **fear not**, for I have found favor with God.*

LUKE 1:30

WEEK 32

*I will **fear not**, for I have received good tidings of great joy, which were given to all people.*

LUKE 2:10

WEEK 33

*I will **fear not**. I will put my trust in God and He will make me whole.*

LUKE 8:50

WEEK 34

*I will **fear not,** for the very hairs of my head are all numbered.
I am of more value than many sparrows.*

LUKE 12:7

WEEK 35

*I will **fear not** the terror that stalks at night
or the danger that prowls in the day.*

PSALM 91:5

WEEK 36

*I will **fear not** bad news; my heart is fixed,
trusting in the Lord.*

PSALM 112:7

Week 37

> *I will **fear not** when I lie down, for my sleep will be sweet.*
>
> PROVERBS 3:24

Week 38

> *Though I am surrounded by a host of my enemies,*
> *I will **fear not**. Even if I find myself in the middle of a war,*
> *I will be confident.*
>
> PSALM 27:3

Week 39

> *Because the Lord has told me not to be afraid*
> *of the words I have heard, I **fear not**.*
>
> ISAIAH 37:6

WEEK 40

*I will lift up my voice with strength and **fear not**.*
I will say to all those around, "Behold our God!"

ISAIAH 40:9

WEEK 41

*I will **fear not** the great multitude that surrounds me*
nor be dismayed; for the battle is not mine, but God's.

2 CHRONICLES 20:15

WEEK 42

*I will **fear not** the faces of those around me for*
God is with me and He will deliver me.

JEREMIAH 1:8

WEEK 43

> I will **fear not** my enemy of whom I am afraid for
> the Lord is with me to save and deliver me.
>
> JEREMIAH 42:11

WEEK 44

> I will **fear not** the words of my enemies nor be
> dismayed when they give me looks.
>
> EZEKIEL 2:6

WEEK 45

> I will **fear not** for Jesus is here and He has touched me.
>
> MATTHEW 17:7

Week 46

Even when I am suffering for doing what is right,
*I will be happy. I will **fear not** any terror*
nor will I be troubled.

1 Peter 3:14

Week 47

*I will not hold my peace. I will speak and **fear not**.*

Acts 18:9

Week 48

*I will be of good cheer. I will **fear not** nor will I be*
troubled for the Lord has assured
me that He is near.

Mark 6:50

WEEK 49

*I will be strong and of good courage. I will **fear not** nor be dismayed because the Lord my God is with me wherever I go.*

JOSHUA 1:9

WEEK 50

*I will be strong and courageous. I will **fear not** nor be dismayed because of the multitude that is around me, for the Lord my God is with me.*

2 CHRONICLES 32:7

WEEK 51

> I will **fear not** the sudden destruction,
> the kind that comes suddenly on the world.
>
> PROVERBS 3:25

WEEK 52

> Because the Lord is here, I will **fear not**, only believe.
>
> MARK 5:36

12 Steps to Living Without Fear

by Lloyd J. Ogilvie

STEP 1:   My fear is really loneliness for God. Therefore, I will claim His promise never to leave or forsake me.

STEP 2:   I will overcome my crippling fears with a creative fear of God expressed with awe and wonder, adoration, and faithful obedience. He is the only Person I have to please.

STEP 3:   I will face my fears, retrace them to their source in my heart, displace them by making my heart Christ's home, and erase them with His perfect love.

STEP 4:   I will let go of my hurting memories of the past, and I will not anticipate the repetition of past pain. I will accept forgiveness from the Lord and forgive everything and everyone in the past—including myself.

STEP 5:   Fear is estrangement from myself. What I fear in others I first fear in myself. Therefore, in response to God's unqualified acceptance, I will embrace myself as worthy of my own affirmation and encouragement.

STEP 6:   I will admit I am inadequate to meet life's opportunities, but I will conquer my fear by becoming a riverbed for the flow of God's guidance, love, and power.

STEP 7: Secure in God's love, I will not surrender my self-worth to the opinions and judgments of others. When I am rejected, I will not retaliate; when I am hurt. Instead, I will allow God to heal me. And knowing the pain of rejection, I will seek to love those who suffer from its anguish.

STEP 8: Today I will turn over the control of my life to the Lord. I will trust His control over what I was never meant to control. With His guidance I will take responsibility for what He has given me to do for His glory and by His power.

STEP 9: I confess my fearful imagination, and today I ask the Lord to make my imagination a channel of His vision and not a breeding ground for fear.

STEP 10: I will face my eventual physical death and proclaim that I am alive eternally. Therefore, I can live abundantly without panic for the rest of my time on earth.

STEP 11: Today, I commit myself to motivating people with love rather than manipulating them with fear.

STEP 12: I will give up the vague idea that given time, things work out. I will boldly face the future unafraid with the sure confidence that God will work all things together for my ultimate good and His glory.[14]

Notes

1. *The Christian's Secret of a Happy Life* 1875 by Hannah Whitall Smith.

2. Ludie D. Pickett, 1897.

3. *The Art of Divine Contentment* 1855 by Thomas Watson.

4. *The Hope of the Gospel* 1892 by George MacDonald.

5. *Imitation of Christ* by Thomas à Kempis (1380–1471).

6. *Till He Come: Communion Meditations and Addresses* by C. H. Spurgeon, 1896 by Charles Spurgeon.

7. *The Imitation of Christ* by Thomas à Kempis (1380–1471).

8. *The Practice of Piety: Directing a Christian How to Walk, that He May Please God* 1636 by Lewis Bayly (language updated).

9. *Till He Come: Communion Meditations and Addresses* by C. H. Spurgeon, 1896 by Charles Spurgeon.

10. *Here I Stand* by Roland Bainton. New American Library for Abingdon 1978, pp 15, 41, 49-50.

11. *The Holiness of God* by R. C. Sproul, Wheaton, Tyndale House, 1985,pp. 106.

12. *Here I Stand* by Roland Bainton. New American Library for Abingdon 1978, pp 30

13. *The New Life: Words of God for Young Disciples* by Andrew Murray.

14. *Twelve Steps to Living Without Fear* by Lloyd J. Ogilvie. Copyright © 1987 by Word, Incorporated. All rights reserved.